WHITTIER ON WRITERS AND WRITING

WHITTIER

ON WRITERS

AND WRITING

The uncollected critical writings of John Greenleaf Whittier

by Edwin Harrison Cady, Syracuse University

and Harry Hayden Clark, University of Wisconsin

Essay Index Reprint Series

BOOKS FOR LIBRARIES PRESS
FREEPORT, NEW YORK

PS
3252
C3
1971
c.1

Copyright 1950 by Syracuse University Press,
Syracuse, New York

Reprinted 1971 by arrangement

INTERNATIONAL STANDARD BOOK NUMBER:
0-8369-2089-9

LIBRARY OF CONGRESS CATALOG CARD NUMBER:
76-128329

PRINTED IN THE UNITED STATES OF AMERICA

CONTENTS

WHITTIER ON WRITERS AND WRITING

None even of Whittier's most lyric nineteenth-century admirers seems to have suggested that he was a major literary critic. In our era of unprecedentedly painstaking and self-conscious criticism, to advance such a suggestion would be to expose oneself to ridicule. Yet his writings about literature, only a fraction of them hitherto available in his *Works*, are worth preservation and attention. Merely by way of conservation of our cultural resources, the whole canon of the writings of every major American author should be made available to the interested general reader, not reserved exclusively for the scholarly specialist who knows how to track down the rarer items. But there are other good reasons for collecting Whittier's literary criticism.

Anyone who wishes to understand Whittier himself must know these writings. Among the shifting lights of the various Whittier myths, we often lose sight of the professional writer working hard against great odds for his self-education. The picture of that serious, life-long student of literature lacks the glamor of the familiar portraits of the barefoot boy, the fiery libertarian, the Quaker saint, the household prophet. Yet the reader, critic, and reviewer must be known before the total Whittier can be understood. The genetic development of his mind, the quality of his daily literary experience, the ideas and intentions which inform his own poetry are all mirrored in these neglected pages.

Whittier was also a working journalist for thirty years, primarily as a reformer. Yet from the beginning, he exploited his literary activities in cultivating a steady view of popular rather than profound criticism. As a man of the people to whom the people eventually gave their cordial confidence, he was producing material rich in meaning for the historian of American taste. His biases remembered, his opinions are unusually significant testimony to the reception, vogue, and general reputation of other writers. His change of tone over the years from strenuosity to a

1

mellow and nostalgic personalism reveals much about the age which canonized him.

Of the writings which directly reflect Whittier's literary attitudes, six were gathered as "Criticism" in the third volume of his standard but decidedly incomplete *Prose Works*. Perhaps twelve more essays in the three volumes may be called criticism. Yet more than seventy essays and reviews have lain unused and well-nigh forgotten, for the most part in rare and scattered files of periodicals, until they were gathered here. Clearly these writings express both the attitudes which remained firmly dominant in Whittier's mind all through his long life and those which were important only at one or another of the different periods of that life.

As Quaker, reformer, and man of his age, Whittier inevitably subordinated all other concerns to moralism throughout his critical career. Fashionably fascinated by Byron in the 1820's, he struggled to subdue his admiration for the sublimity of Byron's genius in order to warn "the young and uncontaminated"[1] against him. From that point forward he praised the healthfully moral and Christian, regardless of literary demerit. Persistently he recorded his objections to loose, lurid, or impious writing. This was the feeling which made him toss his gift-copy of *Leaves of Grass* into the grate, just as it made him exalt the otherwise third-rate work of Brainard, the Carey sisters, Grace Greenwood, and Frances Willard.

If Whittier had no apology to make for moralistic literary judgment, he was sharply aware of the dangers both to critic and author of the other dominant vice of the age—sentimentality. E. P. Whipple's critical contempt for "unmanly puerilities...affectations and sentimentalisms" brought hearty applause from Whittier. Still, the appeal to the heart, a skillful touch upon the tender chords "of our better sympathies," always won him. He hoped the appeal was to true and manly sentiment. If it was to sentimentality and won him anyway, that was to be regretted.

---

1. The quotations here are all taken from the writings reprinted in this volume. They can all readily be found by reference to the table of contents, where they are chronologically arranged and subject-labelled.

2

Another enduring trait of Whittier's poetic self always amazed and rather intrigued him. Pacifist by everything he held dear, physically frail and a semi-invalid for years at a time, he was often creatively impelled to the balladry of action, conflict, and violence. As a critic, also he revelled in literature celebrating heroism, adventure, escape. Scott's "glowing narrative" and in Cooper the "breathing and wild realities" of the sea-tales and the "thrilling narrative of bloodshed and excitement" of *The Last of the Mohicans* gave him almost the delirious joy of an adolescent. Even at the height of his abolition warfare Bayard Taylor could inspire him to write:

> Blessings on the man who invented books of travel for the benefit of home idlers! the Marco Polos, the Sir John Mandevilles, and the Ibn Batutas of old time, and their modern disciples and imitators! Nothing in the shape of travel and gossip... comes amiss to us, from Cook's voyages around the earth to Count de Maistre's journey round his chamber. When the cark and care of daily life and homely duties, and the weary routine of sight and sound, oppress us, what a comfort and refreshing is it to open the charmed pages of the traveller! Our narrow, monotonous horizon breaks away all about us; five minutes suffice to take us quite out of the common-place and familiar regions of our exper- ience...

Beside these continuously important attitudes, the criticism has much to tell us about changing factors in Whittier's mind. In the years of his literary apprenticeship, he was steeping his mind in the current English and American romanticisms. He exploited his studies by poetic imitation and by writing pretentious little appreciations and estimates for the several newspapers and periodicals open to him. Since his poetic sensibilities were first stirred by Burns, it is not surprising that one of the earliest critical efforts was devoted to white-washing his idol. For the troublesome moral lapses, Whittier suggested "the strongest palliation vice can offer — the blight of disappointment acting on the exquisite sensibility of genius." And over that was laid

3

a deep layer of sentimentality as he pictured a pathetic Scotland mourning too late for her bright, fallen star of genius. The conflict between poet and Quaker which called forth such rationalization over Burns became irreconcilable when he considered Byron. It was possible to believe that Burns was a fundamentally wholesome spirit driven astray by circumstances. But what could be done with the sulphurously defiant Byron? Whittier usually struggled briefly for the honor of poetry and then gave way to moralism. Byron, he decided, united "fiendish depravity with angelic intelligence." Yet "enthusiastic admiration of genius" might never excuse "the allurements to vice and loathsome debauchery, the awful impiety and staggering doubt of the unbeliever" in Byron's verse.

The same conflict affected his modish admiration of Shelley's "intellectual powers" and "enchanting productions," though there was no alluring satanic magnificence in Shelley to make the moralist falter. And the "eternal harping" upon the veneration of Shelley by N. P. Willis and his incipient Bohemians galled Whittier into a mood neither judicial nor Quakerly. "Shelley — Shelley — Shelley. Why, this is abominable," he raged. "Who in the name of conscience wishes to hear so much about Shelley?" Willis's poem "To Venus" he spurned as "one of those stale, hackneyed, unreadable invocations to heathen deities ... classical madness and mock Shelleyism." In 1830 he assailed this melancholy, love-lorn mode as "Love-Sick Poetry." Granted that there may be true values in the love lyric, it must, he insisted, concern itself with the true beauties of woman, not "the frail and perishing beauty of her person," but "her deep and pure feelings—the beautiful light of her intellect—the holy affections, which have assimilated her to the angel intelligences of another and better world." The Willis "mawkish affectation of sentiment" inspired him to the sort of blazing attack he was to become famous for when much greater values were concerned. It seemed "an intolerable—unforgivable offense against decency and sober sense ... The idea of a great awkward fellow, six feet in his slippers, and with a beard on his face, whining in this manner, for all the world like an in-disposed baboon, is the truly sublime of the ridiculous—the *ultima thule* of manhood's degradation." By the next spring, however, this flaming indignation had sub-

4

sided to a dilute and lesser irony; and "A Modern Discovery" ironically scolded "these meddlesome Doctors" who would destroy "the idea of pining away under the influence of the delectable and interesting malady of a broken heart" by diagnosing the ailment as indigestion. By the time Whittier came to publish "The Nervous Man" in August of 1832, he was lightly burlesquing the whole pattern of romantic isolation and melancholy, taking love-sickness as merely a part of it.

As for other English romantics, Whittier reports having read in them but has nothing very serious to say. Conventionally, he admired Scott but remarked that "the magnificence of his prose fictions eclipsed the temporary splendor of his poetry." To prove that poetic unevenness (as in Brainard) is not a fatal defect, he grasped the chance to show what he knew and, repeating himself on Byron and Shelley, pointed out that:

> Southey 'discourses fustian' in his Joan of Arc; and in the midst of his wild dreams of Eastern wonder tells his ridiculous story of Kehama's ride into Hell over nine several bridges. Wordsworth, with all his fine perceptions of natural beauty, and his exquisite philosophy, sinks at times into the most disgusting puerility — the pathos and sentiment of an overgrown baby ... and the author of St. Agnes Eve is mawkish and affected in his Endymion.

The moral problem and critical duty apart, Whittier shows great interest in these early years in such "romantic" themes as Gothic horror, antiquarianism, and local color. Like some of the poems and short stories he wrote during the same years, his criticism reflects a strong interest in the power of carefully manipulated supernaturalism to produce a powerful emotional impact. In one of the dominant literary moods of the day, he felt the lure of the mysterious and awful, of the gruesome, and even of the merely strenuously fanciful. Casting aside the humane for the merely literary concern, he explored one account of demonology as "a melancholy instance of the power of the imagination to kill the body, even when its fantastic terrors cannot overcome the intellect." In such a mood he could even lament critically

5

the lack of Gothicism in Fenimore Cooper. "He has never descended into the mysterious depths of human feeling, to hold communion with passion in its secret prison-house," Whittier wrote darkly, "—to watch over the slowly developed images of love; and to witness the incipient struggles of revenge, gathering like a volcano, materials for a fearful visitation." One cannot help wondering what the bluff, extraverted Cooper must have thought if, as is most unlikely, he ever saw that. At any rate, the idea betrayed Whittier into theorizing that the "perfect novelist" would be a combination of Cooper and of Charles Brockden Brown.

The superficiality of this interest is evident from the fact that it disappeared almost completely from Whittier's work within a few years and that the interest in the celebration of the legends and peculiarities of the New England locale became dominant. Stemming probably from Burns, this interest was, of course, to produce his most popular work. It was featured strongly in "New England Superstitions" which, Whittier said, was written to show that "the delusions of the past still linger around us; and that there is no lack of materials for an amusing and not uninstructive work." He sought to induce other men "to embody and illustrate such passages of superstition, as may be considered in any way peculiar to the New World."

Connected with his localism both logically and as a romantic trait was a firm nationalism. Irritated by British sneers, he wrote in 1829 that American genius had already, "in her infancy," "amply redeemed" all debts of civilization to Britain. America's "destiny of glory" is sure, he added, making the eagle scream its challenge:

> Who is there that looks forward to our future greatness, with 'the unborn ages crowding on his soul,' that does not exult in the birth right of an American, and in the proud recollection, this in my own—my native land?

Turning to literary nationalism, he repeated the oft-chorused affirmation that our writers must yet be great because it is the nature of Freedom to elevate the soul and mature its lofty purposes; and because, "They have looked upon Nature in her exceeding sublimity..." Yet for all his faith and hopes, he found

6

that American poetical achievement justified as yet only "the most animating hopes for the future." American verse in 1829 showed, he thought, that we had much to learn. It was "studded here and there with delicate sentiment and exquisite beauty," but it lacked "the sternness of thought — the concentrated power — the overmastering grasps of the imagination, which alone can fix the mighty conceptions of genius in the eternity of mind."

Willis and his crowd aside, Whittier's nationalism made him praise wherever he felt he could. He ignored the crust of poetic obsolescence about Judge John Trumbull to write a handsome obituary for him in 1831. Inspired by Percival's Byronic strain and suicidal gloom, he exclaimed, "We pity the man who does not love the poetry of Percival!" He complimented John Neal, a follower of Cooper and an international ranter. To Cooper himself Whittier extended high praise, though he tended to take parts of it back again. Beyond the objections to Cooper's non-Gothic psychology already noted, he was one of the first to disparage Cooper's women and to attack the ultra-romantic Indians against whom all the New England legends he loved cried out. Yet he saw in the novels the hand of a master, and found "a rich and rare entertainment, in these splendid productions."

Whittier's literary nationalism was firm, then, but temperate. He did not share the youthful Lowell's scorn for all the "blood-rusted" past. He lamented that poverty made it impossible for American poets to use "the ponderous tomes of learning — the rich and magnificent remains of olden intellect — the jewelry of mind, which flashed out in star-like glory upon the darkness of by-gone days." Still, he rejected passionately the notion that the New World is deficient in elements of poetry and romance. The position which he reached by 1832 and seems to have retained throughout life was positive and prophetic but hardly chauvinistic. "As an American," he wrote, "I am proud of the many gifted spirits who have laid their offerings on the altar of our national literature. I believe them capable of greater and more successful efforts. I would encourage them onward."

1832, the pivotal year in which Whittier turned to the master concerns for freedom and reform which dominated the years of his prime, saw also certain shifts of emphasis in his critical writings. His critical mind became a one-way street. Writing

7

which helped his reforms, by even so little as merely fattening the reputation of an author allied to them, was good writing; all else was useless or worse. He warmly applauded the early Lowell for being "a republican poet who dares speak brave words for unpopular truth." But he held Lucy Hooper and Grace Greenwood to be Lowell's equals because they were equally right. His condemnation of Hirst's *Endymion*, with the garbled quotation which the busy editor was too pressed to check, typifies a great deal of fighting criticism:

> The poem is elaborately wrought, and must have cost the author a degree of mental effort to which its theme appears to us by no means commensurate. Life is too short and too earnest to be wasted upon 'such stuff as dreams are made of, and whose little life is rounded by a sleep.'

On the affirmative side he searched tirelessly for ways of scoring a reformer's point. After praising the work of William H. Burleigh for its devotion to refinement and disdain of the clamorous world, he turned to point out to "our Southern readers" that it proved that abolitionists could be nice people too. Far more convincing was an article glorifying the mulatto Russian, Pushkin, "for the purpose of exposing the utter folly and injustice of the common prejudice against the colored race in this country." And the same purpose was served by the printing of long excerpts from a volume of verses written by a man in slavery which showed, Whittier said, that:

> Something of that inspiration of genius which enabled Haydn to hear the choral harmonies of the "creation"...seems to have struggled in the breast of the poor negro rhymer. Surely there is a spirit in man, and the inspiration of the Almighty giveth him understanding. Even in the slave, cast down from the position which God assigned him...classed with the wares of the merchant... Nature recognizes her Lord, although corwnless and dethroned, and ministers to him in the organ sounds of the pines which skirt his task-field, in the sunset glory which burns upon his homeward path, and in the stars

which shine down upon his humble cabin. It is not even in the power of Slavery to wholly unmake the divinest works of Creation—the Chattel which it lifts upon the auction block is but the mutilated and disfigured image of God.

The article concluded with the admission that the poems were not "remarkable either for originality or artistic skill," but with the apposite question: "Who can say that the glorious natural gifts of Burns, or Milton, would have shown forth more brightly than that of poor George, if, like him, these world-renowned masters of song had been born the chattel slaves of a Carolina planter!"

Not all his passion for freedom was channeled against negro slavery, of course. He admired the "Satanic sublimity," as sketched by Lamartine, of the willingness of Danton and the other French revolutionists to sacrifice all for their ideal of freedom. And he gave vent at once to his abolitionist's disgust with the Mexican War and his Quaker pacifism by remarking that the notorious Reign of Terror was morally no worse than "the slaughter of women and children in the bombardment of Vera Cruz," or the death of "every poor soldier, who bleeds away his life on the ghastly battlefields of our Christian civilization." He castigated Macaulay for selling his services to the forces of reaction in England.

When, about 1850, Whittier's mind gradually grew away from the dominance of reform toward the balance of his later years, there came the development of an individual sort of realism. This seems to have been an amalgamation of his romantic localism, become ruralism rather than regionalism, his Quaker passion for "plainness," and a special view of the nature of reality. It is much to Whittier's credit that, afloat on contemporary literary eddies though he was, he opposed the pretentiousness and false elegance of the current literary gentility. The Quaker notion of "plainness" did not, in essence, demand an adherence to uniformity but to the significant facts in a given situation. Mere fancies, however popular, were ruled out as leading to distortion of view and to eventual disaster. Combined with his peculiar localism, this brand of truthfulness made him worship that side of "reality"

9

which was represented by the poetry of Burns.

Part of the background of this realism was a psychology of emotion and of obvious moralistic motivation which seems today dangerously close to sentimentality. In literature Burns, as against Brockden Brown or perhaps Byron, represented the two sides of that psychology. Burns and his like stood for the homely, plain, genial emotions of the pastoral life Whittier idealized, the legitimate life of feeling on which heaven smiled. The others dealt in the romantically sulphurous and high-pressured passion into which he peeped with a shuddering fascination akin to Hawthorne's. In Byron and the Gothic writers, in the superstitions of a country-side whose deep-dyed Puritanism was at long last washing out, and above all in the negative side of the abstractly dualistic morality inherited from Quakers and Puritans alike, he saw the "Passions" as unholy, black, and poisonous. But in compensation for the abhorrence of generations, they took on an allure which in the earlier period he had felt free to indulge in literature so long as the right was firmly enthroned at the end. Both sides, it should be emphasized, had represented reality.

Now, however, Whittier lost interest in the literature of forbidden passions which had called forth his admiration of Brown and Byron, Susannah Rowson, and the superstitious legends of his country-side. He turned instead to a realism expressed in rural life, "the poetry of Home, Nature and the Affections." He sought "Yankee pastorals" of "American domestic life...hallowed and beautified by the sweet and graceful and tender associations of poetry." Gothicism was to be replaced by "calm, quiet appreciation of the beautiful in common and daily life."

Upon this ideal of a literature providing "rare and healthful entertainment" which could cure imaginations diseased from "too much familiarity with heroics, melodramatic literature, and 'strong writing'," he could begin to build critical standards more useful than those founded on political opinion. He objected to the genteel novel with its subservience to "what is called fashionable society," its "foreign phrases," its distorted characters, its "too much of good things in the way of love-making." Scott's novels all but lost their power to charm. Congruently, though the still later Whittier wrote strongly mystical poetry, he objected also to "the dreamy metaphysics, and far-fetched conceits, and

10

shallow philosophies" of "the metaphysical or transcendental school." He noted with relief that Lowell had "happily overcome a slight tendency to mysticism and metaphysics" and was "no longer afraid of the sharp outline of reality." He began to praise simplicity and directness in style.

Toward the end of Whittier's life, he wrote that American literature had properly begun only with the quiet simplicity of *Thanatopsis* and the "terse realism" of Dana's *Buccaneer* which together

> left the weak imitators of an artificial school without an audience. All further attempts to colonize the hills and pastures of New England from old mythologies were abandoned; our boys and girls no longer figured in impossible pastorals. If we have no longer ambitious Columbiads and Conquests of Canaan, we have at least truth and nature, wit and wisdom, in Bryant's "Robert of Lincoln," Emerson's "Humblebee," Lowell's "Courtin'," and the "One-Hoss Shay" of Holmes.

If this was not quite the realism of Howells, it still called for a sane use of truth in literature, a truth of physical nature and human experience which in Whittier's youth was ignored and transgressed to fill the pockets of dozens of now forgotten authors. It allied him with Emerson, Holmes, and Lowell in much of the best of their theories. And it suggests that a study of the roots of American realism will find at least one firmly imbedded in the soil of the romanticistic devotion to themes of the homely, the domestic, the rural, and the regional.

Whittier had too little to say about craftsmanship, about technical and stylistic criteria of criticism; and much of what he said was off-hand or trite. Some of his observations had interest and significance enough, however, to repay consideration. He held to the ruling contemporary idea of poetic genius, believing in "the divine creative faculty" and in the organic unity of art and meaning: "energy, enthusiasm, beauty, abandonment to the emotions, and...spontaneous adaptation of language and rhythm to their subjects." He was not insensitive to careless or undisciplined literary workmanship. The popular irregular ode of his youth

11

jarred on his ear. It was, he wrote "an uneven, racing thing, for it has no smoothness or regularity, and when read aloud its music is about as pleasing to the ear as that of a Sawmill or a Steam engine." "Imperfect rhymes" he called a "glaring fault." He was hardly a prosodic reactionary, however, for he echoed Bryant's *On the Use of the Trisyllabic Foot* in condemning "the monotonous solemnity of Barlow and his contemporaries — their favorite rhymes..." He liked his diction swift and direct, "terse" is a favorite word; "chaste" is another. Very early, he praised in strongest terms the "strength and boldness," "elements of poetry," "beauty and sublimity," and "austere antiquity" of the prose style of Milton.

Concerning the function and practice of literary criticism, which he did not distinguish from book-reviewing *per se*, Whittier had definite and mature ideas. He objected to reviewing which was "rather an *Art* than a *Science*" and in which the writer made the work reviewed "simply a text for some general comments." He strove to take into account "the best critical authorities" and "the verdict of time" on the one hand and "the right of private judgement" on the other. But he would allow neither of these to block criticism from its rightful function of urging writers toward the path of power and sincerity. At the beginning of his career he wrote:

> The true cause of the imbecility of our poetry is found in the dangerous encouragement which is given to the light flashes of fancy...It is time a more independent Mode of criticism was commenced in this country. Most of our literary periodicals are too timid, in fact too dependent, to give their opinions, with the firmness and regard to truth which are necessary. We are becoming effeminate in everything — in our habits as well as our literature, and there is no one fearless enough to investigate the causes of our weakness and supply the requisite remedies.

Yet characteristically, he rejected altogether the "mean and dastardly spirit of criticism" which harped on "a few minor faults and discrepancies." In this mood he lauded the *Fable for*

Critics "as a specimen of brilliant and good-natured satire and discriminating criticisms," particularly because, he says, Lowell's "serious and generous soul" and "humane heart" show kindly "under the light mask of his critical war-dress." And he reflected a little approbation on himself when he encouraged Lucy Larcom, one of the famous Factory Girls of Lowell, to prevent "the poor niceties of aristocratic exclusiveness" from cheating her of recognition.

In judgement of individual authors, Whittier was in some cases decidedly weak, in others reasonably discriminating. His verdict that Percival was immortal and of national importance seems pitiful now. To claim for Brainard "poems which would have done honor to the genius of Burns and Wordsworth" is, if anything, worse. Other less glaring miscalculations may be excused on the grounds of the seeming impossibility of the book-reviewer's keeping much perspective in his day-to-day work.

To Whittier's credit is the recognition of Lowell as "one of the strongest and manliest of our writers" able "to do for freedom and humanity, and for the true and permanent glory of American literature, all that others less gifted...have striven in vain to accomplish." Less significant, since it was published in 1880, was his high tribute to Emerson as poet and thinker. It took little acumen to find Longfellow in 1850 "one of the sweetest poets of our time," a good antidote for ears "tortured by Browning's burlesque of rhythm." But Whittier was perhaps the first critic to call Cooper to account for his "females" and for his ultra-romantic Indians.

Whittier was not a great critic. Few of his insights have retained validity as criticism. As self-portraiture, however, his critical work takes on significance. It shows him a hard-working writer immersed in the contemporary scene, conversant with the work of dozens of colleagues, thinking and laboring to shape his own world after his ideas. He was no aloof intellectual, no half-buried saint. Striving, often a little inconsistent, over-complex, self-confused, he was yet whole in mind and purpose, possessed of an exalted drive of brain and spirit, and in love with beauty as he knew it. Beyond that, he was a picture of his age in many aspects. The naive psychology which rendered both piety and moralism unwieldy and liable to run aground in the shallows of pettiness and rigid convention, the tendency to emotional indulgence, to reach back nostalgically to the life of rural simplicity and integrity fast dissolving in the swirl of an evolving industrial society—all these were in Whittier because they were in the age. But the joy in heroic adventure, the ready plunge into newness, and the search for realities were too. As for the devotion to reform, the taking on of social responsibility in the light of the realization that in a democracy the man was society, and the determination to shape the world to the form of a strong dream of the good way of life, in those things Whittier, with very few beside him, was the age. He was first of all a writer, and the bringing together of these expressions of his ideas about writing and its place in his world, aside from what intrinsic value they do possess, should help everyone who seeks to understand the man and the world of experience he knew.

E. H. Cady.

SUSANNAH ROWSON

Charlotte's Daughter; or the Three Orphans;
A Sequel to Charlotte Temple; by Susannah Rowson.
Boston, Richardson & Lord. 1828.

We have been pleased with a perusal of this little volume. The characters which its author has introduced to our view are not so strongly contrasted as in some of her earlier productions; yet they sufficiently marked to excite our interest. —Lucy Blakeney is, we think, the nost interesting of the group — the progress of her gentle affections - her brief enjoyment of that happiness, which in the language of our author "is never felt but once" — and her noble resignation to the fearful necessity of quenching in her bosom a passion which could no longer be indulged with innocence, are all described with a pathos and sensibility which is peculiar to Mrs. Rowson.

The death of Montraville, the faithless lover of Charlotte Temple is thus described—

"Franklin hastened towards his mother's apartment, but was met on the stairs by one of his brothers, who had been summoned home from Eton. From him he learnt, that his father lay apparently at the point of death, having ruptured a blood vessel; that his mother had been by his bedside almost incessantly, since the accident had happened, and that the whole family were in a state of the greatest alarm and trepidation.

"As he entered the sick chamber, the closed windows, the low whisperings of the attendants, the odours of medicinal preparations, and most of all, an occasional stifled sob from one of the children, who was permitted to be in the apartment for a few moments, brought home to his bosom the conviction that he was about to become fatherless. He approached the bed. His father lay perfectly motionless and silent, with closed eyes, watched by the partner of all his sorrows, who bent over him like some kind angel, with a ministry unremitted and untiring. An indifferent gazer might have read upon the marble forehead and classic features of the patient, noble and generous feelings, commanding talents — a promise of everything that was excellent in character and desirable in fortune — all blighted by once yielding to the impulse of guilty passion. — The wife and the son saw nothing but the mysterious hand of Providence, visiting with severest affliction one whom they had ever regarded with reverence and love.

"Franklin placed himself near the bed, and pressing the hand of his mother, waited in unutterable suspense the moment when his father should awake. At length he slowly opened his eyes, and fixing them on his son, with a faint smile he spoke, in a low voice, "My dear boy, I was this moment thinking of you. It gives me happiness to remember, how soon you are to be blest with the society of one you love, and who deserves your affection. I have not been so tranquil for years, as I am just now, in this thought. I wish that I could see her. I think I could read in her features the promise of your happiness, and then go to my account in peace."

"Franklin pressed his father's hand. The big tears of mingled love, gratitude and sorrow, coursed down his cheeks. He could not speak in reply. He saw by his father's countenance, that it was too late to comply literally with his request, but in the same moment, it occurred to him that he could almost accomplish his wish, by showing him the miniature of Lucy's mother, which he had playfully taken from her on the day of his departure, and in his haste and alarm, at the sudden summons, had forgotten to restore.

"I have a picture of her mother," said he putting his hand in his bosom, "it is a good resemblance of herself."

16

"He drew forth the miniature, and held it up before his father, who rose up, seized it with a convulsive grasp the moment the light fell on the features, and looking upon the initials on the back of it, shrieked out —

"It is — it is come again to blast my vision in my last hour!— The woman you would marry is my own daughter! —Just Heaven!— Oh! that I could have been spared this!—Go, my son! Go to my private desk — you will there find the record of your father's shame, and your own fate!"

"Nature was exhausted by the effort. He fell back on the bed, supported by his trembling wife, and in a few moments, the wretched Franklin, the once gay, gallant, happy Montraville, was no more."

At the close of the volume we are again introduced to Lucy Blakeney —Years have passed since the death blow was given to her dearest hopes, but she is still an interesting object.

"Last but not the least interesting of the cheerful group which was now assembled around the fireside of the Rector, was Lucy Blakeney. Her beauty, unimpared by her early sorrows and pre-served by the active and healthful discharge of the duties of benevolence, had now become matured into the fairest model of lovely womanhood. It was not that beauty which may be produced by the exquisite blending of pure tints on the cheek and brow, by waving tresses and perfect symmetry of outline — it was the beauty of character and intellect, the beauty that speaks in the eye, informs every gesture and look, and carries to the heart at once the conviction, that in such an one, we behold a lovely work of the Creator, blessed by his own hand and pronounced good."

Mrs. Rowson, has, we believe, been censured for her uniform simplicity of style and scrupulous adherence to the realities of life. She has indeed little to do with the imagination. Her pic-tures, simple and unadorned as they really are, doubtless appear tame and spiritless to those who are satisfied with nothing which approaches the bounds of probability. But there is a truth — a moral beauty in her writings, which harmonizes with our purest feelings —a language which appeals to the heart, not in the studied pomp of affectation, but in the simple eloquence of Nature.

Mrs. Rowson, however, was by no means a faultless writer. — In the volume before us, we could point to many imperfections

17

both in style and incident. It should, however, be borne in mind that it was written while its author was engaged in the daily task of superintending the education of nearly one hundred pupils and that she was at the same time the conductor of that popular paper, the Boston Weekly Magazine.

To the admirers of Charlotte Temple, we recommend this volume. It deserves a place with its predecessor.

Essex Gazette, Haverhill, Mass., May 17, 1828.

THE PROSE WORKS OF MILTON

There is strength and boldness in these writings, which cannot fail to please, even those, who are attached to the smooth and graceful periods of modern authors. They are distinguished by that sublimity of sentiment and loftiness of diction, to which none but Milton has ever attained. —The elements of poetry are scattered in every page, and need but the melody of numbers to fix them indelibly on our memories.

There is much of beauty and sublimity in the following, from the speech for the liberty of the Press.

> "Methinks I see in my mind, a noble and puissant nation, rousing herself like a strong man after sleep, and shaking her invincible locks. Methinks I see her as an eagle muing her mighty young, and kindling her undazzled eyes at the full mid-day beam, purging and unscaling her long abused sight at the fountain itself of heavenly radiance."

The reader, who has become familiar with the austere antiquity of Milton's style, who is able to follow his vigorous flights of imagination, and fathom the depth of his reasonings, will not fail to acknowledge in those writings, the presence of the same unrivalled power, which has stamped its undying seal of remembrance on the readers of *Paradise Lost*.

It is to be regretted that those truly valuable writings have been so long neglected. They need only to be known to be extensively admired.

> "Their power is of the brighter clime,
> Which in our birth has part;
> Their tones are of the world, which time
> Sears not within the heart."

Essex Gazette, Haverhill, Mass., May 24, 1828.

ROBERT BURNS

I find a melancholy pleasure in pondering over the works of this gifted, but unfortunate son of genius. Among these, his letters are not the least interesting — displaying, as they do, the lights and shades of his character, and the natural workings of a strong and untutored mind. They are entirely destitute of affectation, and seem to have flowed from the heart of their author without any effort on his part; yet they are full of originality — bold — vigorous, and occasionally eloquent and powerful. Throughout the whole, there breathes a tone of manly independence — the manifestation of a spirit conscious of its innate worth — a spirit which might be shaken, but not controlled by the elements around it. He indeed paid deference to rank, but it was a deference extended only to those, who united with their legitimate nobility, a corresponding loftiness of mind. He seemed to have been fully sensible of the truth of that maxim, which he has himself so happily expressed—

> "The rank is but the guinea's stamp.
> "The man's the gowd for a' that."

The Earl of Glencairn was his friend — as much so perhaps, as the nature of their respective situations admitted of; but the proud and sensitive spirit of Burns turned in disgust from the presence

19

of one, who could bestow the same attention upon titled ignorance and wealthy stupidity, which he had, by an uncommon act of generosity extended to one, who had nothing but the vigor of intellect to distinguish him from his fellows. "The noble Glencairn has wounded me to the heart," said Burns, after witnessing for the last time, his lordship's degrading deference to rank - "but God bless him, 'though I shall never see him more."

And yet, Glencairn knew not that he had so deeply injured the feelings of his high-minded friend. He was ignorant of that undying jealousy, with which true genius watches over the motives as well as the conduct of its pretended admirers.

The voice of flattery is acceptable to all; but peculiarly so to him, who, sensible of his own dignity and power, is conscious of deserving it. Burns felt all this. He listened with untiring eagerness to every token of admiration, and the voice of praise operated on his spirit, like the trumpet peal on the ear of the warrior. But he could not stoop to baseness for the voice of adulation; or struggle with the sordid or mean of soul for the sunshine of favor. From a contest like this, his strong mind revolted. To every open and manly proffer of friendship he responded with alacrity, and the attachments, which he formed, were lasting as well as ardent. But to woman — gentle, and beautiful woman! — the heart and lyre of Burns were dedicated. The warm and universal admiration, with which she greeted his productions, bore up his mind under the weary load of accumulating misery; and the soft eloquence of her sympathy soothed down the ruffled feelings of a spirit worn and agitated by the contempt and heartlessness of man. Her beauty acted like a spell upon his heart, and came over its darkness and desolation, like the mellow moon-light breaking upon a clouded sky.

He erred — deeply erred — but his wanderings have the strongest palliation which vice can offer — the blight of disappointment acting on the exquisite sensibility of genius. —

> "He longed to love — but a frown was all,
> The cold and the heartless gave him;
> He sprang to Ambition's trumpet-call,
> And back they rudely drave him."

20

Sick at heart, and chilled by the cold grasp of penury, what wonder, that he at length sought some relief from painful reflection? He yielded to intemperance, but not an easy or a willing victim. He stood up for a while in the might of his own proud spirit, and battled manfully with his destiny. But the gloom of adversity fell thicker around him, and in the torturing moments of mental agony, he turned an ear to the syren voice of temptation. He saw his situation — he saw the gulf of utter darkness widening, and deepening before him, but the chains of fascination were around him—strong—terribly strong, and the giant energies of a mighty mind became powerless in their clasp.

"That man," said Robert Bloomfield, in speaking of Burns, "stood up with the stamp of intellect on his brow — a visible greatness." It was even so— but it was long ere Scotland was fully aware of the true nobleness of that spirit, which had arisen amidst her wild hills, to send abroad the beautiful light of its genius to the cottage of her peasant and the palace of her noble. She left him, in his hour of adversity, to struggle with the stormy elements around him, and while a thousand hearts were thrilling to the touch of his inspiration, he was suffered to go down, unsupported and unregarded, to a premature grave. Then, indeed, from the misty tops of Cheviot, to the wild and stormy Orkneys, the voice of her lamentation wailed loud and long, and tears of her gifted and beautiful were lavished over his ashes. But the sympathy of a nation came too late! The tear might fall upon his grave, and the voice of wailing go up around if — the knee of the mighty might press upon its sod, and the hand of the beautiful scatter it with flowers — unknown, and unheeded by the ill-fated slumberer.

G.

Essex Gazette, Haverhill, Mass., Nov. 8, 1828.

SIR WALTER SCOTT

The sudden and universal popularity, attained by the early writings of this distinguished individual, is equalled only by the rapidity of its decline. It is almost without a parallel in the annals of literature. But a few years ago, those writings were lauded in every periodical—the heart of a mighty nation responded to the stirring scenes of Marmion, and the pulse of the young and chivalrous quickened at the wild tale of Roderick Dhu. Their minstrel had turned from the living and the bustling world — he had gone back to the dimness and uncertainty of the past — he had leaned upon mouldering monuments, and paused by the ruined temple, and the deserted altar, in quiet communion with the spirit of olden time. The feast, the tourney, and the tale of enchantment became familiar things in his memory. He knew every legend of his native land; and he loved to associate with her wild glens, and heath clad hills, all that was romantic in history, or wild in tradition. These writings are now neglected—but they owe their neglect to the same master-hand that brought them into existence. — Poetry was not the province of Walter Scott — it cramped his strong genius, and rendered his graphic conceptions of character imperfect and limited. A less vigorous mind might have been fully satisfied with the exalted reputation, which he enjoyed as a poet — but with the intuitive sense of genius, he discerned another sphere of action, and entered upon it, in the proud consciousness of controlling power. He succeeded — the magnificence of his prose fictions eclipsed the temporary splendor of his poetry.

We did not intend to criticize his writings — we could not do it, if we wished — we have not read all that he has written, and probably never shall; but in what we have read we have found much to admire and in a literary point of view very little to condemn. It would perhaps be easy to notice a few minor faults and discrepancies — but there is a mean, and dastardly spirit of criticism abroad, and we have no inclination to follow it. There is something provokingly absurd in the idea of an ignorant and conceited critic attempting to sit in judgement on the outpourings of a gifted mind — ridiculing passages, which for strength and correctness bear the same comparison to his own puny efforts, as the giant Andes do to the mole hills at their base.

But we did mean to say something concerning the moral tendency of his writings. We do not believe that anyone can read the simple story of Mid-Lothian without feeling his heart chastened with purer emotions, and strengthened with a deeper assurance

22

in the final triumph of virtue. On the other hand, several of those volumes, which have been produced with such wonderful rapidity and unexampled success, have in our opinion a tendency to subvert some of the purest principles of christian morality. They breathe a war-like spirit — they carry the dazzled reader back to the stirring days of chivalry, and the engrossing interest of the crusade. Our sympathies are enlisted frequently on the wrong side, yet we cannot avoid it, for a fascination is around us - the fascination of glowing narrative, and masterly delineation of character. The wassail-feast — the Bacchanalian revel — the drunken exploits of profane and licentious cavaliers, are described in a manner ill-calculated to produce a salutary impression on the mind of the reader. We do not impugn the motives of Scott. He has doubtless endeavored to bring forth his heroes, as the faithful representatives of their times; but the darker and more repulsive portions of their character have been softened with the too charitable light of romance.

But strip the hero of the olden time of the gorgeous array of chivalry— throw back the kindly mantle of tradition from his dark and irregular course, and hold him forth to the refined gaze of the present generation, in all his original deformity, and he would no longer be an object of admiration. The fearful lines of his character would be too deeply and darkly drawn— and the young— the beautiful, and the sentimental would turn, with abhorrence, from the narrative of his crimes.

American Manufacturer, Boston, Mass., Jan. 8, 1829

AMERICAN GENIUS

"America is fifty years behind England,in point of mechanical genius," says a late English writer. Indeed! —and wherein does this boasted superiority of Britain consist? Let us examine the important inventions which both nations have produced for the last fifty years, and ascertain which have the greatest claim to

23

inventive genius. —What has England produced during that period which may compare with the rail machine — the water loom, and the steam boat? Whom will she place in competition with Franklin, Fulton and Perkins? These are questions which English vanity will find it difficult to answer.

Until within a few years it has been the practice of British Journals and British Travellers, to sneer at every production of our country, as if the term American were but another name for stupidity and ignorance. Our improvement in the mechanic arts is pronounced worthless by the very men who are now reaping important advantages from them. The insulting query of 'who reads an American book?' has been made by the very periodicals, whose pages have since been adorned with the writings of American authors. Our country is yet in her infancy, but, young as she is, her obligations to Britain have been amply redeemed, by the genius of her citizens. The promise of her childhood is like that of the infant Hercules; and it requires no gift of prophecy to foretell her destiny of glory. Who is there that looks forward to our future greatness, with the 'unborn ages crowding on his soul,' that does not exult in the birth right of an American, and in the proud recollection, this is my own — my native land?

Whittier

Philadelphia Album, April 8, 1829, III, 354

AMERICAN LITERATURE

It is a fact to be regretted that the poetical writers of this country have as yet produced little, which can be considered as certain of surviving the present generation of its admirers. They have indeed scattered the gems of thought and the flashes of imagination around us with lavish profusion, but they have thrown no broad illumination — no sunlike splendor over the dawning of American genius. They have multiplied the slender and unsubstantial fabrics of their fancy, but they have laid no deep foundations and upheaved no massy pillars. Their productions have been like the frost-work of an autumn night — beautiful in the first gush of sunshine; but unfitted to abide the winds and the heat of noonday. They are studded here and there with delicate sentiment and exquisite beauty but they lack the sternness of thought — the concentrated power — the overmastering grasp of imagination, which alone can fix the mighty conceptions of genius in the eternity of mind. We have no Milton to urge the wing of inspiration into the awful regions of eternity, — no Byron to unveil the human heart in its brightest and darkest stages of existence – to lay bare the mysteries of mind, and unite, in one fearful embodying of power, fiendish depravity with angelic intelligence.

The want of strength and boldness in our poetical writers, is not a necessary consequence of their country or education. The proud blood of England's mightiest courses through their veins; their minds have never been shackled by tyranny; they are free as the pure breezes of their hills, and it is the nature of Freedom to elevate the soul and mature its lofty purposes. They have looked upon Nature in her exceeding sublimity — the giant cataract — the kingly river — the mountain soaring under a tropic sky to the regions of eternal winter.

The true cause of the imbecility of our poetry is found in the dangerous encouragement which is given to the light flashes of fancy — the tinsel and drapery of poetry, without the substance. — As proof of this, examine the productions of many of our most popular poets. They bear no evidence of manly and vigorous exertion. They have no character of thought —no deep, engrossing interest to chain down our sympathies and work upon the sterner passions. They are pleasant and familiar, and not unfrequently beautiful, and are accordingly published and lauded from one end of the country to the other. The favored writer has no other ambition than to sustain the character which is thus acquired. He has a goodly portion of the world's praise, and this temporary fame answers his purpose, in all respects, as well as a reputation built up on a firmer basis. Why should he quit his fanciful and flowery path for a darker and ruder pilgrimage? Why exchange his easy and popular style, to make an exhausting and uncertain effort for something more substantial and elevated? Why shut himself from the world, and sacrifice the body to the

25

workings of the soul, for that fame, which is seldom awarded to real genius until the wearied spirit has gone to its last and wakeless slumber?

It is time a more independent mode of criticism was commenced in this country. Most of our literary periodicals are too timid, in fact too dependent, to give their opinions, with the firmness and regard to truth which are necessary. We are becoming effeminate in everything —in our habits as well as our literature, and there is no one fearless enough to investigate the causes of our weakness and apply the requisite remedies.

American Manufacturer, Boston, Mass., July 16, 1829

THE WEPT OF THE WISH-TON-WISH

We are afraid the popularity of our old favorite, Cooper, is on the decline. We certainly read his last production with considerable interest, — but, nevertheless we must say, that to our feeling, it is not a little inferior to much that he has formerly given us. It has not the originality of his ocean narratives. In the "Pilot" and "Red Rover," the hand of a master is visible. Perfectly at home in his descriptions — and copying direct from nature in his delineation of nautical character; he has given the readers of modern romance a rich and rare entertainment, in these splendid productions. The storm on the great ocean, or along the rocks and jagged promontories of a hostile coast - the awful mingling of fierce elements — the firm collectedness of the gallant crew of an unmasted vessel, groaning before the tempest— the calm, unshaken tones of command — the quick and fearless obedience — the reckless and irresistible merriment of the seamen, breaking forth even in the very extreme of mortal jeopardy — the horrors of a sea-fight — with the roar of artillery rolling out upon the black waters, as if in mockery of the great thunders above them— the terrible struggle in an outlaw's bosom between lofty generosity and the desire of vengeance; and his last noble act of resignation; leaving his guilty associates to the enjoyment of his ill-gotten gold— all pass before the reader like breathing and wild realities.

The "Pioneers," too, is a fine production. The character of Leatherstocking, the gaunt, old hunter, was an admirable conception — but he loses some of his attractions in the Prairie. "The Last of the Mohicans," is a thrilling narrative of bloodshed and excitement, but a considerable part of it is unnatural. We dislike Cooper's notions of the Indian character. He makes the wild red men of our forests genuine heroes after the manner of Ossian's. This might have done well enough in the old school of romance, when the principal characters of the story were never allowed to do anything, or say anything, like the living and authentic world; but in this age of plain facts and nature it is not to be tolerated. And then, his tales of Indian sagacity, are altogether beyond the bounds of human probability. They may go current on the other side of the water, (indeed, what strange and improbable story will not, which is said or written of this country!) but the author's countrymen, will, in this instance, deny that he holds "the mirror up to nature." In the place of John Bull's broad stare of wonder, the Yankee feels disposed to laugh outright over the marvellous legend.

Nor do we think Cooper happy in his females. In this last work of his, they seem altogether a burthensome appendage to his narrative. We suspect that his disposition and talents are but ill calculated to give interest to the gentler and more delicate departments of romance. He has studied man, as he appears, not as he really is— he has not mingled his own spirit with that of those around him; but has stood afar off, beyond the fever and excitement of the multitude; and copied, with the ease and security of a painter sketching a quiet landscape, the different objects which passed before him. But he has never descended into the mysterious depths of human feeling, to hold communion with passion in its secret prison-house — to watch over the slowly developed images of love; and to witness the incipient struggles of revenge, gathering like a volcano, materials for a fearful visitation.

Could the metaphysical and searching spirit of Charles Brockden Brown have been united to Cooper's inimitable talents for description of outward and tangible matters, we know not what more could have been requisite for a perfect novelist. The writings of the former were certainly in advance of his age. He had no precedent in his peculiar and remarkable style. He gave himself up wholly to his ideal creations, until he actually felt as he must have done, had he been placed in situations similar to those of his imaginary characters; and he noted down these feelings — analyzed them — traced them to their true origin, and this too, with so much real sincerity and natural truth that his long, and, if viewed apart from these deductions, tedious narratives, are capable of producing an intense interest in the mind of the reader.

There are two or three highly-wrought scenes in the "Wept of the Wish-ton-wish" (by the way we enter our protest against this name —'tis an unchristian and unmouthable cognomination,) which the author has never excelled. The terrible details of Indian ferocity and bloodshed furnished his descriptive talents with materials worthy of their power.

Essex Gazette, Haverhill, Mass., Jan. 2, 1830.

THE INFIDEL

(Thomas Paine)

It is an awful commentary on the doctrine of infidelity, that its most strenuous supporters have either miserably falsified their sentiments in the moment of trial; or terminated their existence in obscurity and utter wretchedness. The gifted author of the "Age of Reason," passed the last years of his life in a manner, which the meanest slave that ever trembled beneath the lash of the taskmaster, could have no cause to envy. Rosseau, might indeed be pointed out, as in some degree, an exception — but it is well known, that the enthusiastic philosopher, was a

28

miserable and disappointed man. He met death, it is true, with
something like calmness. But he had no pure and beautiful hope
beyond the perishing things of the natural world. He loved the
works of God for their exceeding beauty — not for their manifestation of an overruling intelligence. Life had become a burthen to him, but his spirit recoiled at the dampness and silence
of the sepulchre — the cold, unbroken sleep, and the slow wasting
away of mortality. He perished, a worshipper of that beauty, which
but faintly shadows forth the unimaginable glory of its Creator.
At the closing hour of day — when the broad West was glowing
like the gates of Paradise, and the vine-hung hills of his beautiful land were bathed in the rich light of sunset, the philosopher
departed. The last glance of his glazing eye, was to him an everlasting farewell to existence — the last homage of a godlike intellect to holiness and beauty. The blackness of darkness was
before him — the shadow of the valley of Death was to him un-
escapable and eternal — the better land beyond it was shrouded
from his vision.

In Blackwood's Magazine for November, there is an article
concerning the author of the "Age of Reason," which in these
days of progressive infidelity, may induce some, who are as yet
but on the threshold of scepticism, to pause and reflect upon the
fate of one of its ablest apostles. There is a moral in his history,
which is full of fearful warning.

Essex Gazette, Haverhill, Mass., Jan. 2, 1830

FUGITIVE POETRY ... BY N. P. WILLIS

This volume has been pretty severely handled by many of our
contemporaries. We think they have not done the author justice.
There *are* beauties — original and praiseworthy passages in this
collection; and, although like "angel visits," they are "few and

far between," they should not be passed by in a critical notice of the young gentleman's rhymes. We think, nevertheless, that Willis was altogether wrong in publishing the fugitive, and unstudied effusions of his last two or three years. He must have known how much his reputation not only as a poet, but, what is infinitely of more consequence, as a *man;* had suffered from their first and evanescent appearance in newspapers and other periodicals. He *did* know it— he knew the good sense of the community had been shocked by the utter recklessness of moral principle, manifested in too many of his offerings — he knew that the friends of Literature, who had hailed his early efforts, as the dawning of a new sun in the sky of Intellect, —had first doubted — then disbelieved, and finally turned away from his puerile compositions, with mingled disgust and sorrow; and he knew more - over, that the pure and beautiful, who had lingered with delight over his earlier writings, were shrinking back with horror from his licentious page. They had knelt down to worship a familiar Angel, and they had risen up with trembling, for an unholy spirit was before them.

God forbid, that we should quarrel with Willis, for writing poetry, (thankless and unprofitable as the task, or pleasure of it, may be,) for we acknowledge, with due humility, that we have been foolish enough to attempt as much, ourself, for which sin we hope to be forgiven by the public. We do not blame him for indulging himself in the fascinating clime of Poetry—we have not a heart to do so— but we *do* blame him for leaving the pure and better path, in which his journey was commenced, for one forbidden and unhallowed, and totally unworthy of his real genius. We blame him for degrading his gift of mind; for prostituting the resources of an immortal intellect, to the lowest shrines of earth— for his boyish vanity and affectation, at a time, when he should stand up in the strength and dignity of manhood, conscious of his responsibility to his Maker and to his fellow-men.

The volume now before us, is, as a whole, inferior to his "Sketches," published two or three years ago. The "Shunamite," a scripture sketch is the first article; and no-wise remarkable for beauty or strength; but the "Scene in Gethsemane," which follows it, is really beautiful. "Contemplation" is a poor affair, very sentimental, and very foolish. The "Sketch of a School-

fellow," is pretty poetry, in the Wordsworth style. We pass over
a mass of indifferent matter —and turn to "Psyche at the Tribunal
of Venus." This is really excellent; and is worthy of any American writer. Of the "Table of Emerald" we might say the same.
Take the following from the latter, in proof:

> "There was one dark eye — it hath passed away!
>   There was one deep tone —'tis not!
> Could I see it now—could I hear it now,
>   Ye were all too well forgot.
> My heart brought up, from its chambers deep,
>   The sum of its earthly love;
> But it might not— could not-- buy like Heaven,
>   And she stole to her rest above.
>
> That first deep love I have taken back,
>   In my rayless heart to hide;
> With the tear it brought for a burning seal,
>   'Twill there forever bide.
> I may stretch on now to a nobler ken,
>   I may live in my thoughts of flame—
> The tie is broken that kept me back,
>   And my spirit is on, for fame!"

"The Declaration" is supremely ridiculous. —"Isabel" is no
better; and "Mere Accident" is worse — it is scandalous. We
should not wish the author any greater punishment than to be
under the necessity of reading this delicate piece of composition
to an audience of intelligent and sensitive females. What a pretty
figure Mr. Nathaniel Pettingill Willis must have made while
assisting the matchless Viola in the romantic operation of washing her feet! —And then, too, he had

> ——"a cousin's kindness for her lip,
> And in the meshes of her chestnut hair
> He loved to hide his fingers."

According to his own story, the author of this volume, moves
among his female acquaintance, with the fickleness of the wind,

31

that "*kisses* everything it meets."— He is a lucky Epicurean, that is certain — and the ladies, — dear creatures — how *very* obliging they are!

The lines "To a Bride" are very fine — the last stanza in particular.

> "Pass on! there is not of our blessings one
>   That may not perish—
> Like visiting angels whose errand is done,
> They are never at rest till their home is won,
>   And we may not cherish
> The beautiful gift of *thy* light— Pass on!"

We have not room for any long extracts, else we should like to give our readers a few specimens of Willis's best efforts. His faults, and he has many, we hope will be rectified hereafter. He is yet young; and he may easily retrace his steps. He has been treated with severity— his talents have been greatly underrated— but a vigorous effort on his part, will reestablish his reputation, in the eyes of the literary community.

Essex Gazette, Haverhill, Mass., Jan. 9, 1830

PERCY B. SHELLEY

A correspondent of the American Daily Advertiser, has undertaken to defend the character of this man from the charges which we made against it a short time since in an article headed "Infidelity." The writer styles himself the friend of Shelley, what kind of a friend he does not tell us, — but probably of the infidel rather than of the poet — and then goes on to quote from our article, and deny our statements.

He objects to the word "dissipation" as applied by us to his "friend." What was it but dissipation, or something worse than dissipation, in the common acceptation of the term, which led him to steal away the pure affections of an innocent school-girl,— a child, unpractised and uninitiated in the duplicities and hollow-heartedness of the world— to carry her away from her friends—to pervert and poison her mind with those vile sophistries, which, under the pretext of elevating the character and establish the "rights of woman," degrade her from her high place of purity, and render her a suitable companion for the accursed of Heaven? In this instance the wretched victim awoke to a sense of her degradation;— she perished by drowning, and, in all probability a suicide.

The writer speaks of the "virtuous wife" of Shelley. This wife was the daughter of the licentious, the profligate and shame-less Mary Woolstoncraft!

He next quotes us incorrectly. By substituting the word "brow" for that of "soul," he is enabled to furnish us with the following paragraph:

"He died, as he had lived, with a cloud upon his brow, and the seal of infamy upon his memory." What presumption! what gross and insulting mockery! *who* is there that shall say how *he* died, who perished in the solitude of the whirlwind? Who is there that can declare with what fear, or with what fortitude, he encountered the dark horror of the destroying tempest?"

That Shelley *did* perish, "with a cloud upon his soul," let the beautiful lines which he wrote just before his death, bear testimony. We would insert them in this place if we had a copy of them at hand — but we dare not trust our memory, although their affecting sentiment is indelibly fixed therein. As to his fear or his fortitude in the terrible moment of his death, we know nothing. The eye of that God, whom he denied, was alone upon him, in the thick tempest.

We have said thus much, in justification of our remarks. It is no pleasure to us to dwell upon the errors of the departed. No man can think more highly of Shelley's intellectual powers, than ourself — none can be more enthusiastically fond of his enchant-ing productions. But mere Genius shall never take the precedence of Virtue, in our estimation. We cannot worship the forms of

Vice and Licentiousness, — although the glowing drapery of an
angel may be gathered around them.

Essex Gazette, Haverhill, Mass., Feb. 27, 1830

POEMS BY AN AMERICAN

Henry Pickering

American poetry has of late assumed a definite and peculiar
character. The strength and dignity of the old school of American writers have given place to lighter productions, in which
brilliance and eccentricity of thought and diction, are the dis-
tinguishing characteristics. We confess that we are pleased with
the change. The monotonous solemnity of Barlow and his contemporaries — their continual sacrifice of sense to rhythm — the
perpetual recurrence of their favorite rhymes, are sufficiently
irksome to account for our preference of modern poetry. We know
very well, that as yet, no American writer has built up for himself that proud reputation, which has distinguished so many sons
of song in the old world — we know that as yet our most promising
poets are but on the threshold of the temple of immortality; and
we know, too, that the time is yet far distant, when their literary
labours will be substantially   remunerated by our matter-of-fact
and money-getting population. Our writers are aware of the latter
fact, and hence their light and ephemeral effusions. They dare
not give themselves up, in the stern devotedness of martyrs, to
the pursuits of literature, for they know that neglect and penury
must necessarily follow the attempt. They have, in truth, no
leisure, no respite from the routine of daily exertion for sub-
sistence. They cannot immure themselves in the quiet of their
study, among the ponderous tomes of learning — the rich and magnificent remains of olden intellect — the jewelry of mind, which

34

flashed out in star-like glory upon the darkness of bygone ages. They cannot *labour* upon their productions, with the sustaining hope, — the almost visible certainty, of future fame, — of future emolument, cheering them in their toil, and beaming like a star of promise, through the anxiety and the gloom of years. If they write at all — it is at stolen moments — at intervals of transient leisure and abstraction from the worldly and commonplace business of life. They have neither leisure nor desire to polish their hasty productions, but send them abroad with all their imperfections — with beauty wedded to deformity.

But enough has been done by our poetical writers to justify the most animating hopes for the future. The materials are rapidly accumulating for the establishment of a national literature. Already our first writers have in a good degree thrown off the fetters of servile imitation; and are beginning to think and act for themselves.

The volume before us, — a thin and modest duodecimo, — is from the pen of Henry Pickering, Esq. This gentleman has been considerably abused by some of our conceited critics; but seldom has abuse been more undeservedly applied than in the case of this writer. He has indeed little of the brilliancy and glitter which distinguish a considerable portion of the writings of our most popular poets. But there is a uniform sweetness and delicacy in his verse, perfectly congenial to the feelings of sensitive and retiring genius. Like Bryant, he seldom astonishes by the wild and irregular introduction of a splendid thought, flashing like a solitary diamond amidst the coarse and common earth; — and his taste seems to have led him to dwell upon the loveliness of nature; and the influence of the milder and gentler feelings of humanity, rather than upon the darkness and storm of the one, and the fierce passions of the other. He loves to paint the exquisite tints of the sunset cloud, and the arching of the rainbow; but he attempts no sketches of the over-hanging tempest, when the whole heaven is one tossing sea of vapour, and the quick lightning is abroad on its errand of vengeance.

The manner in which this volume was published, is perfectly in accordance with our ideas of the author. He did not publish for money — hardly even, for reputation as a writer; — but for the satisfaction of himself and a few of his friends. Only twenty-five copies were printed.

We give an extract from "The Hudson" —It is a beautiful passage of rich description:

Has the sun drain'd thy founts?
Or hast thou swerv'd from thy majestic course?
As proudly onward sweep thy waves to day,
As when thy mighty springs were first unlock'd,
To swell the exulting main! But where are now
Thine ancient honors? Where thy boundless wood
And sea of leaves? O'ershadowing hill and vale
Magnificent! —The daring man who urg'd
Erewhile, his prow adventurous through thy deep,
And s aw, shoot like a meteor o'er the tide,
The Indian skiff, and wild eyes peering out
The densest shades, beheld thee, wonderous Stream!
In all thy grandeur. Mountains that beneath
Thy undiscoverable depths once stretch'd
Their giant feet, then far in the blue heavens
Precipitous rose with their incumbent woods;
And lofty verdurous tufts, more beautiful
Than aigret upon Soldan's diadem,
Crown'd each bold crag: while from thy northern founts,
Even to the ocean's brim, dark forest spread,—
Which waving with the evening breeze or morn's,
Alternate threw their broad continuous shade
O'er half thy watery realm.

Essex Gazette, Haverhill, Mass., Mar. 27, 1830.

JEFFERSON'S RELIGION

We have noticed of late in several papers, a few extracts from the writings of the illustrious Jefferson, which, are supposed by many to contain a direct avowal of the principles of modern

36

Infidelity. We acknowledge that the extracts will admit in some degree of this construction. But we do not believe that they express correctly the real opinions of their author. They are the fruits of vague speculation — nothing more. We regret, however, that they have been permitted to see the light. They have offered a pretext for an attempt to substantiate old and half forgotten charges — for fixing the stigma of infidel depravity upon the memory of the illustrious dead. They are calculated to call forth the imprecations of the religious zealot, and the applauses of the abandoned infidel.

But, whatever may have been his speculative belief, Thomas Jefferson was not a practical Infidel. He respected and loved the free exercise of rational religion. He was not the bigot of an exclusive creed; but his spirit rejoiced at the privilege which those around him enjoyed, of worshipping their Creator according to the dictates of their own consciences. We publish, in support of our assertions, the following letter. It is the answer he returned to an epistle from his friend Canby, a member of the Society of Friends.

Sir— I have duly received your favor of August 27th; am sensible of the kind intentions from which it flows, and truly thankful for them, the more so, as they could only be the result of a favorable estimate of my public course. During a long life, as much devoted to study as a faithful transaction of the trusts committed to me would permit, no object has occupied more of my consideration than our relations with all the beings around me, our duties to them and our future prospects. After hearing and reading everything which probably can be suggested concerning them, I have formed the best judgment I could, as to the course they prescribe; and in the due observance of that course, I have no recollections which give me uneasiness. An eloquent preacher of your religious society, Richard Mott, in a discourse of much unction and pathos, is said to have exclaimed aloud to his congregation that he did not believe there was a Quaker, Presbyterian, Methodist, or Baptist, in Heaven — having paused to give his audience time to stare, and to wonder, he said, that in Heaven, God knew no distinction, but considered all good men, as his children and as brethren of the same family. I believe with the Quaker preacher, that he who steadily observes those moral

37

precepts in which all religions concur, will never be questioned at the gates of Heaven, as to the dogmas in which they differ; that on entering there, all these are left behind us; the Aristideses and Catos, Penns and Tillotsons, Presbyterians and Papists, will find themselves united in all principles which are in concert with the reason of the supreme mind. Of all the systems of morality, ancient or modern, which have come under my observation, none appear to me so pure as that of Jesus. He who follows this steadily need not, I think, be uneasy, although he cannot comprehend the subtleties and mysteries erected on his doctrines, by those who, calling themselves his special followers and favorites, would make him come into the world to lay snares for all understandings but theirs; these metaphysical heads, usurping the judgment seat of God, denounce as his enemies, all who cannot perceive the geometrical logic of Euclid in the demonstrations of St. Athanasius, that three are one, and one is three, and yet that three are not one, nor the one three. In all essential points, you and I are of the same religion, and I am too old to go into inquiries and changes as to the unessentials. Repeating therefore my thankfulness for the kind concern you have been so good as to express, I salute you with friendship and brotherly love.

Essex Gazette, Haverhill, Mass., April 17, 1830.

LORD BYRON

Since the publication of Moore's Life of Byron it has become fashionable to avow an enthusiastic reverence for the genius and character of the noble bard. The most unqualified censure is heaped upon those who have spoken freely against Lord Byron's infidel principles; —who have dared to lift their voices in solemn warning against the baleful fascination of his licentious numbers. This practice is unjust — uncharitable and dangerous — dangerous because it confounds all creeds and all practices,— because in its enthusiastic* admiration of genius — its idolatry of poetry — the allurements to vice and loathsome debauchery, the awful impiety and the staggering doubt of the unbeliever, are either forgotten or passed over as the allowable aberrations of an intellect, — which had lifted itself above the ordinary world, which had broken down the barriers of ordinary mind: and which revelled in a creation of its own — a world, over which the sunshine of imagination lightened at times with an almost ineffable glory, — to be succeeded by the thick blackness of doubt and terror, and misanthropy, relieved only by the lightning-flashes of terrible and unholy passion.

Byron was an infidel — a wretched infidel. The blessings of a mighty intellect — the prodigal gift of Heaven, became in his possession a burthen and a curse. He was wretched in his gloomy unbelief; and he strove, with that selfish purpose, which the miserable and unprincipled feel, to drag his fellow beings from their only abiding hope — to break down in the human spirit the beautiful altar of its faith; and to fix in other bosoms the doubt and despair which darkened his own. We *pity* him for his early bias towards infidelity; but we *condemn* him for his attempts to lead his readers — the vast multitude of the beautiful, the pure, and the gifted, who knelt to his genius as to the manifestations of a new divinity — into that ever-darkened path, which is trodden only by the lost to Hope — the forsaken of Heaven — and which leads from the perfect light of holiness, down to the regions of eternal Death.

If ever man possessed the power of controlling at will the passions of his readers that man was Byron. He knew — he felt the mightiness of this power — and he loved to exercise it — to kindle in a thousand bosoms the strange fire which desolated his own. He loved to shake down with a giant's strength the strongest pillars of human confidence; to unfix the young and susceptible spirit from its allegiance to virtue, and to the dearest ties of nature. No man ever drew finer and more enchanting pictures of the social virtues; and Love and Friendship never seem more

*Compare the remainder of this and the succeeding two paragraphs with the article "The Nervous Man," pp. 104-105. Whittier must sometimes have been hard pressed to meet his deadlines.

beautiful than when made the subject of his vivid and heart-touching sketches. But a cold sneer of scepticism—an unfeeling turn of expression—or a vulgar and disgusting comparison associated with images of purity and loveliness, like a foul satyr in the companionship of angels — breaks in upon the delicious reverie of the enthusiastic reader, and the holiness of beauty departs— the sweet spell is broken forever, and the sacred image of virtue is associated with disgust and abhorrence. It seems as if the mighty magician delighted in adorning with the sun-like hues of his imagination the Paradise of Virtue, in order to discover more fully the fell power which he possessed of darkening and defacing the fair vision, — of sending the curse of his own perverted feelings to brood over it like the wing of a destroying angel on his errand of desolation.

What for instance can be more beautiful — more deeply imbued with the genuine spirit of pure and holy love than the epistle of Julia to her lover in Don Juan? Yet to whom are these holy sentiments attributed? To a vile and polluted paramour — an adultress;-to a bosom of glowing not with the etherial principle of love, but with the fires of a consuming and guilty passion. They should have emanated from a heart as pure as unsullied as the descending snow-wreath, before one stain of earth has dimmed its original purity. Yet it was Lord Byron's glory — the very acme of his triumph — to bring the virtues and the vices of our nature to a common level - to put into the mouths of the criminal and the licentious the words of truth, and holiness, and love.

We are not insensible to the surpassing power of Byron's genius. He was the master spirit of his time. We feel that we are not competent to sit in critical judgment upon the outpourings of his lofty mind;—but we thank God for having given us a perception, faint and imperfect it may be in comparison with that of others, but still to us a valuable perception, of the pure and beautiful in nature and intellect. And, governed as we are in our remarks by this perception, we feel that we are only acting the part of our duty, in warning the young and uncontaminated against an enthusiastic reverence for the productions of Lord Byron.

Essex Gazette, Haverhill, Mass., May 8, 1830.

FALKLAND

(Bulwer Lytton)

This is the first of a series of romances known by the name of
the "Pelham Novels." The author writes with uncommon power—
his sketches of real life are graphic and amusing—his tales of
passion, vivid, and full of engrossing interest. There are passages in "The Disowned" and "Devereux" which no living
novelist has ever exceeded—passages of extraordinary beauty—
full of high-toned and magnificent Poetry; and illuminated by the
sunshine of a beautiful philosophy. But it is not of these we
would now speak. Falkland, from whom the story takes its name,
is a gentleman of fortune —misanthropic from early disappointment—
a proud, melancholy being—just such an one as a romantic woman
would fall in love with. He introduces himself into the family of
a parliamentary gentleman, absent at the time, and contrives to
fall desperately in love with—who think you, reader? —a daughter,
or a sister, or a country cousin of the gentleman?— No such thing.
His love is fixed upon the mistress of the family— upon the wife
of the absent legislator. And this love is reciprocated—and is
consummated by—adultery!

We dislike the book—we condemn it unqualifiedly. Its tendency
we are sensible will be pernicious. How can it be otherwise? The
sympathies of every man, woman, or child who reads it will be
given to the lovers. We admit there is a moral in the sequel of
the story but there is *poison* in the passionate elequence of
Falkland. It is not in human nature to resist such appeals as
those of the seducer—it is not in man to resist such love—such
wild fondness as that of the seduced. By this deep and all-
absorbing devotion of the lovers, we are prepared to execrate
the officious lady who marred the fine plot which they had concerted; and to join with the author of the story in heaping fierce
anathemas upon her. We learn to hate the sober-minded husband—
to despise those who, in the least, interfered with the unhallowed
and accursed intercourse between the guilty pair. Let us not be
told then, that *such* writings subserve the cause of Virtue. Love
is a pure, holy, and etherial principle—Passion, licentious and
and unlawful passion, is low and brutish and sensual. Let it not

then be dignified with the name, and knelt to in the character, of Love.

New England Weekly Review, Hartford, Aug. 2, 1830.

AUTHORSHIP

BY A NEW-ENGLANDER

(John Neal)

This is John Neal's last novel—or book, rather—and, take it "for all and all," it is a most singular affair. We have read it carefully through, but we cannot feel ourselves satisfied that we have discovered the meaning of the author, if indeed, he *had* any meaning. It is wild, rambling, and, to our conception, unnatural. It has beautiful passages—gems scattered here and there, in apparently unpremeditated and careless profusion—magnificent ideas, flashing out from the midst of disconnected and unmeaning paragraphs, like diamonds scattered upon the 'cold, grey earth,'— beautiful by the contrast. But it is not a good book—we don't believe John Neal thought it was, when he handed it over to the publishers. It is unreadable—and, with a great deal of truth, and a great deal of beauty, it will not do the author much credit. It is not worthy of the author of "Otho," or of Rachel Dyer, the commencement of which is full of magnificent poetry.

The story is told in the pleasant and egotistical style which is so familiar and agreeable to the author. He is his own hero— and a queer one he is too. He represents himself as a real "native Yankee," full of wonder, while visiting, for the first time, the Abbey of Westminster—the sepulcher of England's mightiest. He here meets with two strangers—a man and a woman—and is wonderfully pleased with the latter—in other words, he falls in love with an unknown woman—one whom he had seen only in the dim and mysterious twilight of the Abbey—under circumstances, to say the least, somewhat suspicious. We should give our readers an outline

of the story, if it were possible—but, in truth, the story, if it
deserves the name of one, seems only intended to connect, in
some degree, the fine descriptions—the odd philosophies—the innumerable digressions of the writer. We will content ourselves
with copying the following beautiful description of Portsmouth,
in England.

"So I set off on my pilgrimage from Ryde,[1] after running down
to the pier for the fourth time, to look at the Portsmouth shore as
it lay glittering afar off through the thin haze and over the smooth
beautifully-shadowed sea, like a sort of aerial panorama.—Stop,
reader—I must try to give you a notion of Portsmouth as it appeared to me at the time I speak of, whether you have or have not
stood upon the pier at Tyde, while the waters were spread before
you like a sheet of changeable satin—changeable with shadow and
light and with every hue between the deep yellow of the shore
and the deep strange blue of the sea—I must—I must—whatever
may become of my story, my heroine, or myself. Two or three
nights before, I had been struck with the amazing beauty of a
sunset, which I saw from the Portsmouth side—it was like the
sunsets of North America; not so brilliant however, nor dyed
with such exalted and fervent hues, but *like* them in the stillness
of their beauty, when to look at them is enough to bring the
water into your eyes and to make your heart run over—especially
if there is a woman at your side. I grew melancholly, and I thought
how very little we know of each other in this world, nations of
nations, neighbours of neighbours, brothers of brothers. On every
side of me was the proof; on every side of me beauty and power
that were considered peculiar to America; a real Indian-summer—
that Sabbath of the whole year; a superb sunset, and huge trees
overloaded with foliage that appeared like a sort of gorgeous
blazonry. Their colors were not so vivid as we have them in
America, nor so various, nor did they overhang all the mountain-
sides, and all the rocks, and every foot of the earth as far as
the eye could reach, with a sort of ponderous and fluctuating
shadow; but they had a beauty of their own, a beauty that we
never see in the New-World, a sort of pomp which is not the pomp
of the wilderness, and a sort of wealth which is not the wealth

1. Ryde, or Ride, on the Isle-of-Wight, opposite Portsmouth.
(Whittier's note)

of our everlasting woods, but graver and quieter. They swell up
to the eye, cloud over cloud, with colors that we love to see in
a picture. Not so with our savage North-American landscapes—
they would startle and scare you if they were painted with fidelity. If you had gathered your ideas of nature from Claude or
Poussin or Hobbima, or Both, or Ruysdal, or from any body that
ever painted a landscape in Europe, you would never be able
to endure the truth in a landscape in North-America. The bright
blue, the deep firey crimson, the scarlet and gold, the orange
and purple, the innumerable shades of brown would appear unworthy of a picture. You would feel as men who have been brought
up to the stage do, when they see the terrible passions at work
off the stage—you would swear that Nature herself was unnatural.

"So much for the sunset which I had seen two or three nights
before; but nothing that I saw then, though it was all that I have
described it to be, could equal the view that I had now of the
Portsmouth shore off Gosport, of the shipping, of the military
works, and of the far blue sea with a fleet riding slowly over the
dim barrier which hardly separated it from the far blue sky—
launching away, ship after ship into the unfathomable air, as if
they knew, like the huge birds of South-America when they float
over the top of the Andes—*into* the sky—with all their mighty
wings outspread, that there was no power in heaven or earth
able to wreck them, or shatter them, or disturb them on their way.
It was a picture to be remembered for life—to be carried away
on the heart, as if the colors were burnt there, and the moveable
beauty of a camera obscura had been shut up for another day, or
melted into the material and fixed there for ever and ever.

"The broad-striped waters were like a smooth satin, glossy
with light, and rippling with a low soft air that stole over the
green surface like a shadow. You could see it move. They were
green too--of a beautiful positive green, such as I never saw any
where else; no doubt owing to the mixture of a sober yellowish
dye produced by the sands near the shore with the cold blue of
the ocean—a blue that appeared as black as midnight, where the
waters were very deep. On every side of me were happy faces—
grown-up children wading about on the shore, and looking as if
they had never heard the name of sorrow, as if to them life were
but one long holiday; barges and wherries dipping to the swell;

44

great ships at anchor with their sides turned up to the air as if they had been cast away in the very middle of the great deep; and others afar off towering into the sky like prodigies, or floating up and fading away, like so many superb, creatures of the air, each abroad on some particular errand of its own.

"The night before there had been a gale, which prepared the way for what I saw now. I stood on the pier and saw it approach-- the breeze sounding over the deep, the mist rolling toward me like a heavy white smoke, the tide moving with a steady roar, which grew louder and louder as it heaved and weltered underneath our feet; and the Portsmouth shore, while it seemed very high and very far off, breaking through the mist with an effect such as I never saw before, either in pictures or in sleep. The sky was cloudy—it was even dark—there was nothing above able to produce what I saw, nothing of brightness in that part of the above which I could see; and yet the high lands of the opposite shore, lands that were neither high nor picturesque when the wind was another way, were gleaming with a sort of mysterious beauty, such as you may conceive would be the character of a fine painting, if it were covered with a grey gauze and lighted up from within. It was what I should call, if I were not afraid of being charged with affectation, a *sketch* by the Deity, a shadow of the landscapes that we are to see hereafter; so faint, so ethereal was it, so unlike the landscapes of our earth."

Here is a sample of the author's accurate conception of the human heart. It is truth, boldly and plainly told. We *are* by nature thus selfish. The feeling which is here described is a familiar thing to every bosom.

"I saw that she could not bear the idea of parting with me; I saw that she would be miserable after I had gone whatever she might say, and so, much as I loved her, I was all the happier for it. Strange! I would have died for that woman—I would, upon my life—and yet I could not bear the idea of being forgotten by her, though I knew that if she remembered me, it would make *her* life a burthen to her. Such is love—such the very nature of man! Love as we may, we never love another so much as we do ourselves, even though we destroy ourselves to make that other happy—it would kill us to know that one we care for could be happy without our help."

Critics may talk as they please—but for ourselves we *do* like the bold, vigorous, and erratic style of Neal. We could fall asleep over the delicately rounded period and the studied and labored paragraph, but the startling language—the original idea, standing out in the bold relief of all its native magnificence, rouse up our blood like a summoning trumpet-call.

New England Weekly Review, Hartford, Aug. 9, 1830

PERCIVAL

We pity the man who does not love the poetry of Percival! He is a genius of Nature's making—that singular and high-minded Poet. He has written much that will live while the pure and beautiful and glorious, in poetry and romance, are cherished among us. His aim has always been lofty—up—up—into a clearer sky and a holier sunshine—and if he has failed at all, he has failed in warring with the thunder-cloud, and crossing the path of the live lightning. His "Prometheus" is a noble poem. —There is no affectedness about it—all is grand and darkly majestic—it has a few soft and delicate passages—no tinge of the common love-poetry of the day—no breathings of vows to "rose lipped angels in petticoats,"—no dalliance with a "lady's curls." He left *such* things to the dandies in literature—to our love-sick and moon-struck race of rhymers, and went forth in the dignity and power of a man—to grapple with the dark thoughts which thronged before him, moulding them into visible and tangible realities.

The apostrophe to the sun, in this poem, we have ever looked upon as the most magnificent specimen of American poetry within our knowledge. The following stanza is of unrivalled excellence;

> Thine are the mountains, where they purely lift
> Snows that have never wasted, in a sky
> Which hath no stain; below the storm may drift
> Its darkness, and the thunder-gust roar by,
> Aloft in thy eternal smile they lie
> Dazzling but cold: thy farewell glance looks there,

And when below thy hues of beauty die
Girt round them as a rosy belt, they bear
Into the high dark vault a brow that still is fair.

The American Monthly Magazine in a fine notice of Percival hints that he is forgotten by the public. It is not so. In every village of our country, where the light of Literature has penetrated, the name of Percival is familiar—and the beautiful language of his poetry is breathed from the soft, rich voice of woman, and upon the bearded lip of manhood.

New England Weekly Review, Hartford, August 9, 1830

WILLIS'S MONTHLY MAGAZINE

Good, bad and indifferent—all mixed and compounded together—tessellated and incongruous—a strong original sentiment coupled with one which has been bandied about like a football for centuries—a nervous thought linked with a weak, puerile, or affected one. Such is the aspect of the present number of the American Monthly.

We will examine the first article—a well conceived poem, by the editor—"The Dying Alchymist." 'Tis a noble subject. There was something almost unearthly in the patient and searching spirit of the Alchymist of the olden time—a spirit that never grew weary with its toil, which never faltered from its purposes—undeterred by the mockery of man—unquenched by the bitter waters of disappointment. It was a strange idea, that of changing the gross and duller metals into untarnishing gold, and of discovering an elixir so potent as to renovate the bowed form of age—to light up again the sunken eye of expiring humanity; and to give to the wrinkled brow, and the fallen cheek, and the attenuated and tottering form, the purity, the freshness and the voluptuous moulding of exquisite beauty. Yet for these objects, more than

47

one tall spirit has toiled for years, with a dim eye and a trembling hand, over the poison mineral and the noisome drug—watching the mutations of compound after compound, agitated alternately by delirious hope and fear, and unutterable disappointment. The commencement of the poem before us is very fine—stronger too, and happier, than anything else which we have seen from the pen of the author.

> "The night-wind with a desolate moan swept by,
> And the old shutters of the turrets swung
> Screaming upon their hinges, and the moon,
> As the torn edges of the clouds flew past,
> Struggled aslant the stained and broken pane
> So dimly, that the watchful eye of death
> Scarcely was conscious when it went and came."

And the conclusion is also beautiful. After having described the death of the Alchymist, the author says—

> "And thus had passed from its unequal frame
> A soul of fire—a sun-bent eagle stricken
> From his high soaring down—an instrument
> Broken with its own compass. He was born
> Taller than he might walk beneath the stars,
> And with a spirit tempered like a god's,
> He was sent blindfold on a path of light,
> And turned aside and perished! Oh how poor
> Seems the rich gift of genius, when it lies,
> Like the adventurous bird that hath out-flown
> His strength upon the sea, ambition-wrecked—
> A thing the thrush might pity, as she sits
> Brooding in quiet on her lowly nest."

"Pencillings by the Way." Tolerably good—quite spirited—but vastly indelicate. Willis writes for the ladies—he hints in his Editor's Table that the dear creatures are writing letters to him of congratulation and admiration, etc. God forgive the man, for his vanity no less than for his impudence. *Such* writings as his "Pencillings," are unworthy a place in a lady's parlor. They have the licentiousness and hardihood of Byron's without the redeeming qualities of originality and genius.

Here comes one of those stale, hackneyed, unreadable invocations to heathen deities. "To Venus"—forsooth! Why that same Venus has been poetized by every generation of rhymers from the time of the blind man of Scio down to the date of the last American Monthly. Venus—friend Willis, who *is* Venus? Either say nothing of her, or spread her beautiful history before your readers in the shape of an ode—not forgetting her assignation with Mars—her flirtations with Bacchus, and a score of other delicate matters;—and pray represent her, as the ancients of Elis did, riding on a goat with her feet on a tortoise—a fine posture, truly!—and, by way of variety, describe the peculiarly modest ceremonies which characterised the worship of her votaries. For shame, Willis! Do let the creature alone—and if a correspondent whines about her again, send him the New-England Weekly Review. It is an unfailing antidote for the kind of classical madness and mock Shelleyism which pervades the epistle "To Venus." Do our readers wish for a specimen of the epistle? Well—here it is.

> "Leaving the poor green blades to look--alas!
> With dim eyes at the moon—(ah! so dost thou
> Full oft quench brightness)—Venus! whether now
> Thou passest o'er the sea, while each light wing
> Of thy fair doves is wet—while sea-maids bring
> Sweet odors, for they—(ah, how foolish they!)
>   They have not known thy smart!
> They know not, while in ocean caves they play,
>   How strong thou art."

Yet here *is* a specimen of fine poetry, and the only passage deserving even the name of poetry in the piece; yet it serves to show how the author *might* have written, had he chosen a decent subject.

>   "Thou at whose quiet pace
> Joy leaps on faster, with a louder laugh,
> And sorrow tosses to the sea his staff,

And pushes back his hair from his dim eyes,
And looks again upon forgotten skies;
And avarice forgets to count his gold."

"About Letters, etc." Shelley—Shelley—Shelley. Why, this is abominable. Who in the name of conscience wishes to hear so much about Shelley? This eternal harping of Willis and his correspondents about Shelley and his writings, is enough to rouse in wrath the gifted and ill-fated bard from his cold slumberings beneath the eternal ocean.

"The Prisoner for Life," by James O.Rockwell. 'Tis strange— 'tis passing strange—there is nothing in philosophy, analogy, ethics, or the fitness of things, to account for the fact--that Rockwell and Gates and Daniels—three as fine fellows as ever snapped a 'grey goose quill,' in the face and eyes of the public, should be given over to Jacksonism. It must be that they admire the old General's literature, and that of his immaculate cabinet. But we were speaking of Rockwell's poetry—here are two stanzas —all we have room to copy.

"When the summer sun was in the west,
    Its crimson radiance fell,
Some on the blue and changeful sea,
    And some in the prisoner's cell.
And then his eye with a smile would beam,
    And the blood would leave his brain,
And the verdure of his soul return,
    Like sere grass after rain.

But when the tempest wreathed and spread
    A mantle o'er the sun,
He gathered back his woes again
    And brooded thereupon:
And thus he lived, till Time one day
    Led Death to break his chain.
And then the prisoner went away,
    And he was free again."

"The Parthenon," by Park Benjamin. Rich and graphic poetry—such as we should expect from the author of "Nineveh."

Now comes the Editor's Table, and barring its affectedness, it is quite a good paper. The notice of Hillhouse we are pleased with. "Hadad" is a wonderful creation of genius;—a poem which will be read and admired long after its author has ceased to walk with the living. And this is immortality—the immortality of genius. For this poor boon—the admiration of posterity—does the eagle spirit toil and suffer—the eye grow dim with its midnight vigil, and the brow roughen with its lines of thought, and the warm heart wither with the intensity of feeling. For our own part, we would ask nothing of posterity. We hope not—ask not-an influence in the future—in the goings on of the great world after we shall have gone to our last slumber. 'Tis an idle and foolish dream—this yearning after a name to dwell upon the lips of unborn generations. We would have Fame visit us now—in the freshness and springtime of our existence—when we could share its smile with the friends whom we love,—but we ask not a niche in that temple, where the dead alone are crowned—where the green and living garland waves in ghastly contrast over the pale cold brow and visionless eye; and where the chant of praise and the voice of adulation fall only on the deafened ear of Death.

New England Weekly Review, Hartford, September 27. 1830

LOVE-SICK POETRY

"I sings her praise in poetry—for her at morn and eve
I cries whole pints of bitter tears and wipes 'em with
my sleeve."   Anonymous

We are weary—disgusted—and ill-natured in contemplation of the subject before us. —This eternal rhyming to cheek and eye and head-gear—this mawkish affectation of sentiment—this profanation of the purity and holiness of love—this detestable imitation of the Irish voluptuary, without a particle of his inspiration—is enough to drive one, whose nerves are less delicate than our own, into absolute madness.

Do the authors of these ridiculous productions suppose they are really complimenting the objects to whom they address themselves? We know enough of human nature to assert fearlessly that no lady ever felt flattered by them—ever received them with pleasure, unless the standard of her intellect was far below mediocrity. Who that possesses the delicacy of feeling so inseparably associated with our ideas of woman, *could* feel a moment's thrill of pleasure, at the low and hackneyed tribute to the color of her cheek or the wreathings of her tresses? We will not think thus lightly of woman. We cannot degrade her by supposing for a moment that she *could* be flattered by a homage which was limited to the frail and perishing beauty of her person—which knew not; and recked not of her deep and pure feelings—the beautiful light of her intellect—the holy affections, which have assimilated her to the angel intelligences of another and better world.

There is indeed a surpassing charm in the perfection of female beauty. But it is only when the *mind* and the *heart* shine through the dark lustre of the eye, or leave a legible and beautiful language upon the cheek—or lend a deeper music to the rich voice, that the outward impress of beauty can be deeply and lastingly felt. Unillumined by the spirit, the most perfect form is but a cold and desolate temple. —Like an ice-berg glittering in the light of sunset, with the rainbow hues of beauty, it may dazzle for a moment, but none may dream of communion with its frozen sterility.

We repeat it, we are weary of this rhyming about love, and kisses, and dimpled cheeks, and raven tresses. It is an intolerable—unforgivable offence against decency and sober sense. That any one who has the least pretensions to manhood—any one save a sentimental school-boy, at that important crisis in his *teens* —

> "when his fingers begin
> To feel the soft down that comes over his chin,"

should perpetrate any thing of the kind, is to us perfectly unac-

52

countable. The idea of a great awkward fellow, six feet in his slippers, and with a beard on his face, whining in this manner, for all the world like an indisposed baboon, is the truly sublime of the ridiculous—the *ultima thule* of manhood's degradation.

New England Weekly Review, Hartford, September 27, 1830

LEXINGTON AND OTHER POEMS

(Wetmore)

This is the title of a beautiful volume from the pen of Prosper M. Wetmore, Esq. It is full of strong and nervous poetry. There is nothing of affectedness about it—but a clear, healthy spirit runs through the book. Not that we consider *every* piece in the book worthy of its place—but we speak of their general tone. There is a "song" which has no business there—and a "Sonnet to Mrs. Hemans" which is no better than it should be. "Lexington" is indeed a noble poem. We thought so when it was first published—but it has been severely and closely revised, and is now every way worthy of its magnificent subject. "The Return" is plaintive and beautiful. "The Appeal" has a high merit apart from its poetical beauty. —In denouncing the unhallowed spirit of military Ambition the author has done honor to his heart as well as to his intellect. Too long has this spirit gone abroad to desolate and lay waste the earth. Too long has the multitude knelt down before its presence as to an idol. Let the veil be torn away—even with a rude hand, from that abominable idol; let the cruelty and the bloodshed which surround it be revealed; and its worshipers would turn from it with the disgust and abhorrence of men, who had offered up vows of love at the feet of a veiled skeleton.

We have no room for extracts or we would gladly make them. The volume is beautifully printed—beyond any thing of the kind which we have seen from the American Press—and in consideration of its beautiful typography and its yet more beautiful poetry, deserves a place alike in the ladys' *boudoir,* and the library of the scholar.

New England Weekly Review, Hartford, October 18, 1830

ATLANTIC SOUVENIR FOR 1831

We have looked over this beautiful annual with much satisfaction. In typographical neatness—and in the durability and beauty of its binding, we find a decided improvement from the ordinary style of 'getting up' these autumnal visitants. The engravings are many of them of the highest order. "The ship wrecked Family" is a very striking representation of the odd confusion incident upon a sudden transfer from a ship's cabin, to a cabin on land, surrounded by the motley articles secured from the wreck.

"*The First Born*" is an interesting tale by Richard Penn Smith, Esq. of Philadelphia. The effect of personal deformity is well delineated—an effect, which, however natural it may be, is nevertheless cruel to the unfortunate and misshapen creature of humanity. There *is* a revolting of the heart—a sickening sense of disgust--in our intercourse with the deformed, —which too often imparts to our conduct an air of cruel and undeserved scorn. It should not be thus. The temple which God has filled with a portion of his own Eternal Spirit, should never be despised and spurned at, however unseemly may be its proportions.

"*Infancy,*" a poem by Frederick S. Eckard, is unequal to some other productions which we have seen from the same pen, and yet beautiful. '*Couleur de Rose,*' is newspaper poetry. '*The Winds*' by Hannah F. Gould, of Newburyport, is a fine production. There is a beauty of rhythm, and a vividness of language in the following, beyond the ordinary contributions to a Souvenir.

> "Ye mark, as we vary our forms of power,
> And fell the forest, or fan the flower;

54

When the hair-bell moves, and the rush is bent,
When the tower 's o'erthrown and the oak is rent;
As we waft the bark o'er the slumbering wave,
Or hurry its crew to a watery grave;
And ye say it is we, but can ye trace
The wandering winds to their secret place?"

'*The Eve of St. Andrew,*' by J.K. Paulding—a well told story of Indians and Frenchmen. Paulding is a popular writer—but his *forte* is in humorous description and polished satire. In the seriously told tale before us, he has however been very successful.

The '*Song*' which follows is a miserable attempt at poetry and sentiment. Why--we reject communications to the Review every week which are decidedly superior to it. '*To Laura*' by Frederick S. Eckard is little better.

'*The Passion Flower,*' by J.H. Bright contains some fine verses. '*Three Score and Ten*' from the pen of C.W. Thompson, a young gentleman who has written some beautiful poetry for the Annuals of the last two or three years, is not remarkable for beauty of style or incident.

'*A day in New York a century since*' gives us a view of the scenes and fashions of the renowned city of Gotham, through the dim twilight of a century. '*Brandywine,*' by Miss E.M. Chandler, is full of strong and vigorous poetry, of the Childe Harold stamp.

'*The Hour of Rest*' is illustrated by a beautiful engraving-- but the poetry is pitiably common-place. '*The Grave-Lamps*' is a beautiful poem by S.M. Clark, of this city. It alludes to a custom among the Chinese of placing lamps once a year over the graves of deceased friends. We give a specimen.

A beautiful and holy rite!
Thus flinging o'er the dead,
A lustre like a living light,
To crown the lost one's bed.
It seems as if pure fire from heaven
Had fallen as of old;
As if some burning cloud were riven,
And there its fragments roll'd
Or why should man e'er cast a pall

Of gloom above the grave?
For flowers will bloom, and sun-light fall,
And winds their pinions wave,
Alike on grave or pleasant bower,
On mountain or on glen,
And clouds which seem o'er graves to lower,
Rise from the hearts of men.

The 'Dead of the Wreck' is a horrible story of shipwreck and cannibalism, by W.L. Stone, Esq. A crew of unfortunate wretches are cast upon the desert island of Anticosti in the Gulf of the St. Lawrence, in the depth of a wild and stormy winter, without provisions, and without any means of escaping from the inhospitable region. The following extract is a fearful description of the demoniac effect produced by extreme hunger. The finer and better feelings of humanity depart—and a savage appetite—a beastly yearning for blood—alone absorbs the faculties of the mind.

There were indications, too, that I was not the first
to struggle against the horrid idea;

The brows of men, by the despairing light,
Wore an unearthly aspect;

their eyes glared wildly upon each other, with fierce demoniac looks. Their teeth and hands were often clenched convulsively, and they would sit for a long time fixed as statues, their haggard countenances bent sullenly upon the earth. Those in their hammocks would groan, and gnaw the wood, and chew their wretched covering. Some began to rave and curse, while a few, submissive, gloomy and silent, sunk down in immovable and unutterable despair. One or two became delirious and frantic, their piercing maniac cries evincing the the keenest suffering of body and mind. And some were still glaring upon each other with fixed, dead, unrelenting eyes.

'*The Urn of Columbus*,' by Lydia H. Sigourney is strong, elevated, and original—but somewhat obscure. 'When the old world her infant sister spied' is a splendid line. '*Stanzas*' by N.P. Willis. We did hope to find something better from the pen of this young gentleman. 'Tis a foolish, mock-sentimental affair, 'redolent' of 'tears,' 'love' 'frozen nerves' 'bright lips,' 'despair,' etc. It is strange that a *man* should seriously perpetrate such things—that a spirit like that of Willis should be content to hover like a weak-winged bird over the low and familiar things of Earth, when, like the 'sun-bent-eagle,' it might bear up with a strong pinion against the overhanging tempest—front the burning eye of the sun, and cross the path of the living thunder.

Giles Heatherby, or the *Free Trader*, by G. Wallace. This is a well-told story—somewhat too long for an annual, however.

Hymn of the Cherokee Indian, by I. M'Lellan. This is a plaintive and beautiful production. —There is something inexpressibly affecting in the idea of the Indian's departure from his birthplace. View the subject as we may, the present policy of our government towards the unfortunate Cherokee, is one of unparalleled cruelty. It is the breaking up of the long established quiet of home—the uprooting of all the affections which gather around the place of nativity. The few remaining remnants of a once mighty people have been driven back from the great sea and the broad rivers of their old possession—their forests have been shorn away; and the lurking places of the deer, the moose and the beaver have been broken open. And we are driving them onward without ceasing. A few years more, and "the places which once knew them shall know them no more:" and, where the council-fire shone over the war-dance, and the Powwah knelt to the Great Spirit —

> "Their bow of strength lie buried with the calamut
> and spear,
> And the spent arrow slumber, forgetful of the deer."

Beresina, by T. Fisher. Newspaper poetry—rhymes—common sense—and no originality. *Time*, by Dr. M'Henry, of Philadelphia, is respectable poetry. The Doctor has written some good things in his life-time—better than people have been generally willing to allow—but he is not remarkable for originality or strength.

A Story of Shay's War, by Miss Sedgwick. —We know of no female prose writer, if we except the gifted author of "Hobomok," who may compare with Miss Sedgwick. But the sketch before us is certainly very far from her best style. The "Shays Insurrection" is a fine field for the novelist or story-teller. There are a thousand ludicrous or pathetic incidents connected with it, which might be moulded to advantage in the hands of genius.

Morning among the Hills, by C.W. Thomson. This piece has been already published in half the papers in the country. It is a respectable poem—nothing more.

The Brahmin's Curse, is the title of a beautiful poem by Mrs. Louisa P. Smith, formerly of Boston. But for a few exceptions it would deserve the first place in the book. Its author is quite young—and we are satisfied she will yet do honor to American literature.

The Spirit's Dwelling, by W. Leggett, Esq. This gentleman has written some good articles of poetry—the one above mentioned included—but his talents appear at best advantage in his prose productions. His "Sea Sketches" are amusing and graphic.

We have thus gone over the Souvenir. As a general thing we may say that the engravings are good—the prose nervous, spirited and original—the poetry below mediocrity. In fact many of the rhymes would disgrace even a Jackson newspaper.

New England Weekly Review, Hartford, October 18 and 25, 1830

THE TOKEN FOR 1831

We are pleased to handle these annuals—to finger their delicate gilt-edged leaves—to pore over the gems of thought, scattered profusely through their pages; but we object to their appearing at such an unseasonable time, —it is "eating the feast before feast day." They are intended for new-year's and Christmas gifts and tokens, and the public have the perusal of them long before they can be applied to the use for which they were intended. Before "the merry Christmas" comes, their contents are copied and recopied all over the union. Every thing that is good in them is dressed up for the public in every variety of type, from *Pica* to *Minion*, and published in every paper in the country, from the village hebdomadal to the city daily—from the "Memphremagog Intelligencer" and "Quampeagan Republican," even to the "New York Mirror" and "Philadelphia Album"—and if one would make a present of these books to his mistress, he can give her nothing but the second course--there will be nothing *new* to her in them; she has read and reread them, and they are almost unfit for the purpose the publisher designs them for, and have nothing to recommend them but the engravings and the binding. The solid fare is then all stale, and the embellishments, the spices and the jellies are all that are palatable. Let the publishers look to this, and send forth their annuals at the proper season; let them keep their feast until feast day, when we warrant them, their bill of fare will find more admirers, and (what is of greater consequence,) more purchasers, than if produced a month before every other annual. There now seems to be a sort of strife between them, whose works shall appear first, and the consequences are as injurious to themselves as to those who use them as mementos or tokens of affection.

The three first engravings in the *Token* are decidedly the best that have ever appeared in a Boston work, but they do not equal those of the *Atlantic Souvenir*. The presentation plate, drawn by G. Harvey, and engraved by E. Gallaudet, represents a fountain surmounted by a basket of flowers. The only objection that we could have in our heart to make, is, that it is too fine, too soft and too delicate. Mr. Gallaudet is a young artist but will undoubtedly, if he pursues the path he has marked out for himself, at no distant day rank high in his profession. *"Just Seventeen"* engraved by Cheney from a painting of Sir Thomas Lawrence, is excelled only by *"Mine Own"* in the last *London Souvenir*, which if our memory does not fail us, is the only female head we have ever seen that excels the one in the *Token*. The *title page* is equal to any thing that has yet appeared of the kind whether English or American. The heads in the centre, (by Gallaudet,) are surpassingly beautiful—the drawing of the flowers rather stiff and mannered, but the beauty of the engraving, (by V. Balch, of N.Y.) is sufficient to make ample amends.

"The Mysteries of Life" is an eloquent paper by the Rev.

59

Orville Dewey. We have always admired the works of Mr. Dewey, and seldom feel such an inclination to bow down to the majesty of mind, as when we are engaged on his writing. By the most intense application and severe study he has matured his mind on almost every subject, and fervent and impassioned thoughts flow forth from the immortal fountain, at the touch of his master wand, like waters from the rock of Horeb. —But it is with reference to the high and responsible duties of a minister of the gospel, that his studies have been chiefly pursued; and his writings are always calculated to lift the thoughts of the reader above the grosser things of earth—to contemplate and admire the incomprehensible mysteries of Infinite Goodness. In the beautiful paper in the *Token* he has put forth in strong and glowing language the "Mysteries of Life" and points out with impassioned eloquence the wisdom and goodness of their Author. Though every "chamber" in his figurative hall of life may be "inscribed *Mystery*," and be unopened to the many, his vigorous mind seems to possess the key to unlock at least a part of them—to search the hidden stores of wisdom and bring to light the treasures that are accessible to but few--to shadow in bold relief the higher and holier purposes of life, and bring man to bow down before the wisdom that contrived them.

"*To a city pigeon*" is a smooth and flowery poem. It is unacknowledged, though undoubtedly written by Willis, who certainly need not be ashamed of it, for it would add to the fame of any writer. "*To the Moonbeams*" by Hannah F. Gould, is characterized by the author's usual free and easy versification. —The last verse we particularly admire: —

> "Away! to the slope of the dew-bright hill
> Where the sod is fresh and the air is chill,
> Where the marble is white and all is still;
> But never reveal who there is led
> By your light, to mourn for the early dead,
> And weep o'er the lost in her lonely bed."

"*The lost Child*" is an admirable engraving by Gallaudet from a painting of Fisher's. An indistinctness in part of the left hand of the picture where the figures are placed, and the outrageous form of the wolf are the only faults that can be found with it. It is illustrated by some poor, newspaper verses by "O. W. H." "To ⏤" by ⏤ a poor sonnet. ⏤There *may* be some meaning to the lines, and the author *may* have had an object in writing them, but we confess we can discover neither.

"*The Religion of the Sea*" is a fine article by F.W.P. Greenwood. Though it has nothing original in design to recommend it, yet the writer's thoughts are expressed in such chaste and elegant language, the attention of the reader is irresistably chained to them. He treats of the "great and glorious sea" with the hand of a master. Its storms and tempests, its calm and sunshine—the low murmur of its unquiet waves, when the palm of its Maker's hand is upon it, hushing the waters, or the loud roaring of the mighty billows as they dash up in armies against the eternal rocks only to have

"their fury dashed to air—"

the whisperings of the breeze, as it wanders, like a spirit of the deep, "over the whole bright host of waters" or the war of the angry winds when "the storm spirit comes in his wrath"—are portrayed in rich and beautiful language, and rise up before the reader's imagination in all their awful grandeur or quiet beauty, with ten-fold force and distinctness from the writer's polished sentences. One vulgarism we notice and cannot but think it a misprint. It struck us with the more force, like a flaw in a diamond, from its being elsewhere so perfectly polished—

"They teach us something of our unrevealed connexion, something of the unseen and unimaginative future, and if *so be that* we are disposed," etc.

"*Sights from a steeple*" is a pretty article, indicating more power than the writer has here thought fit to put forth. As a confirmation of our remarks and a proof of the versatility of his powers, we give the following detached passages.

"I see vessels unlading at the wharf, and precious merchandise strown upon the ground, abundantly as at *the bottom of the sea, that market whence no goods return, and where there is no captain or super cargo to render an account of sales.*"

"How various are the situations of the people covered by the roofs beneath me, and how diversified are the events at this moment befalling them! The new-born, the aged, the dying, the strong in life, and the recent dead, are in the chambers of these many mansions. The full of hope, the happy, the miserable, and the desperate, dwell together within the circle of my glance. In some of the houses over which my eyes roam so coldly, guilt is entering into hearts that are still tenanted by a debased and trodden virtue, −guilt is on the very edge of commission, and might be averted; guilt is done, and the criminal wonders if it be irrevocable. −There are broad thoughts struggling in my mind, and, were I able to give them distinctness, they would make their way in eloquence."

"The clouds, within a little time, have gathered over all the sky, hanging heavily, as if about to drop in one unbroken mass upon the earth. At intervals, the lightning flashes from their brooding hearts, quivers, disappears, and then comes the thunder, traveling slowly after its twin-born flame. A strong wind has sprung up, howls through the darkened streets, and raises the dust in dense bodies, to rebel against the approaching storm. The disbanded soldiers fly, the funeral has already vanished like its dead, and all people hurry homeward−all that have a home; while a few lounge by the corners, or trudge on desperately, at their leisure."

"Lake Superior" by S.G. Goodrich. Bold and original. The following verse is unrivalled in its way−

> "*The gnarled and braided boughs*, that show
> Their dim forms in the forest shade,
> *Like wrestling serpents seem*, and throw
> Fantastic horrors through the glade."

"Lines" by L.M. ——t,−rather pretty, but not good enough for an annual. "*American Scenery*" is an engraving by G.B. Ellis, from a fine picture by Cole in possession of D. Wadsworth Esq. in this city. The lines "*Cora's appeal*" overstrained and foolish. It is but one page from the sublime to the ridiculous.

"*The fated Family*" by Grenville Mellen we will wager our right hand, though his name does not appear with it. If it is not him, it is, as the yankee said of his wooden nutmegs, "a good

62

imitation." It is a good story, well told, and worthy of Mellen. Need we say more? "Remembrance" by Charles West Thompson, not worthy of the author of *"The American Eagle"*. *"Ronda"* by the author of "A year in Spain," we have not read, and will not, with some sage guardians of our literature, *McGrawler* like, review works without reading them. *"A Thought"* by P.M. Wetmore-- unworthy of the author.

"Ode on Music," by Grenville Mellen. We have an aversion to these irregular odes.--Their unequal lines and rhymes jar discordantly on the ear; but the one before us is crowded with beauties, and, we are sorry to say, not a few faults. It has all Mellen's strength and power and will undoubtedly add to his fame, but it has also his imperfect rhymes, which have of late become a glaring fault in his productions.

The following is perfect, save in rhyme.—*Turned* will not rhyme with *wind*, notwithstanding the author has tried to make it. This evidence of haste or carelessness is becoming more and more common in Mellen's writings, we notice it particularly in his "Age of Print."

> "He heard it 'mid the trees!
>   Where forth in thought he hied
>   Under the eventide,
> *Where flowers were closing on the drowsy bees*
>   Then, as in dreamy mood he turned
>   His linked fancies wild,
>   He heard, far up, as one afraid,
>   The music by the shrill leaves made—
>   Then shouted, as a child,
>   To that lone harping of the wind!"

On the whole we cannot but like it, though sorely against our wish it is to like such an uneven, racing thing, for it has no smoothness or regularity, and when read aloud its music is about as pleasing to the ear as that of a Sawmill or a Steam engine.
"I meet them in my dreams" by Miss Louisa P. Smith—decidedly the best thing of the kind we have seen. "The Haunted Quack" by Joseph Nicholson, we recommend to all lovers of fun. It is a good

story, told with infinite humour—we would "analyse it" as the hero, the haunted quack, Hippocrates Jenkins said, but we have not room. "The Midnight Mail" by H. F. Gould, is not equal to the same writer's lines "To the Moonbeams."

"Lines" by nobody.

"Just Seventeen." The two first verses are good, but as a whole, it is not what should have accompanied so fine an engraving. "Te Zahpahtah," a sketch from Indian History by the author of "Tales of the Northwest" is a short sketch of the disastrous consequences following the introduction of whiskey to an Indian camp. The liquor is brought in, gratuitously distributed to the savages, and the most riotous scenes occur. The father falls by the hand of his son, and the son is slain by the hand of the father —brothers are armed against brothers, until the oldest and most respected chief of the tribe is killed. The effect upon the noble and high-minded savage—the degrading and humiliating consequences of intoxication, are portrayed in a forcible manner. The deadly effects of "the supernatural water," as the Dahcotahs called the liquor, did more in days gone by, towards exterminating the Indians, than did any other weapon of our forefathers. It set them in hostile array against each other—it divided the family against itself—and, to use their own emphatic language, came down upon the race like a curse from the Great Spirit, and made them fools.

"Return to Connecticut" is a beautiful poem by Mrs. Sigourney. This gifted writer never succeeds better, than when her pen is employed in honoring the land of the pilgrims. "The New England Village." This is a well-told story. We dare not hazard a guess at the author's name, but why in the name of all that is wonderful, did he not acknowledge it? It is worthy of any American writer. Plain language, telling a plain story with every appearance of truth, is a rare thing as times go.

"The birth of Thunder" by J. Snelling is one of the most perfect pieces in the book. It is an illustration of a legend of the Indians, which says that the great Thunder Spirit had birth "about twenty eight miles from the Big Stone Lake. As soon as the infant Spirit could go alone, it set out to see the world, and at the first step placed his foot upon a hill about twenty five miles distant, a rock, the top of which actually seems to bear the print of a gigantic human foot."

"The Indian's burial of his child" by Mrs. Sigourney does not please us as well as her "Return to Connecticut," though it bears evident marks of the master hand.

"The Adventurer" supposed by the editor of the Token to be written by John Neal, and purporting to be the *real* life of John Dunn Hunter, the man, who, a few years since, created such a stir among the knowing ones, with an account of his sufferings and hardships among the Indians. It is Neal's work, fast enough. His peculiarities are stamped so plain upon it, that he who runs may read. It is in his most pleasing style, and we only want to be assured that it approximates to the truth to relish it highly.

"To —" a fine poem. It is enough to tell the name of the author, O. W. B. Peabody.

"To a lady on her thirtieth birthday" by — worthy of the author. "Isabel" engraved by Danforth, painted by Newton, verses by nobody. The engraving is good, but the picture execrable—a great strapping wench leaning on a five rail fence, or something of the kind, with a child's head and arms like a mountaineer's —"The Village Musician" by James Hall, editor of the Western Souvenir, is the best story of its class we have seen for months.

"Lord Vapercourt, or a November in London." The title is enough—we shall not read it, for we are reviewing what is supposed to be strictly an American work. "Farewell" by — would disgrace the veriest rhymer that ever gingled words with a piece of chalk on the smooth side of a board fence. A specimen--

"Say, hath the lip no other bliss
Than words to give? O yes, O yes,
For one more near than friend or brother!
There! There! Another! O, another!

"The Captive's dream" is a fine poem, by S. G. Goodrich. "Mary Dyer" is a simple tale by Miss Sedgwick. Without a plot, without any extraordinary excitement, the attention of the reader is irresistibly chained to the story. Miss Sedgwick has told of the sufferings of the martyr and her consolations in death in such plain, but captivating language, we venture to say, none will ever begin the tale and leave it unfinished. We are glad to see the story of Mary Dyer thus made familiar to the youth of our country. It will warn them of the rock upon which our ancestors, with all their virtue and religion, were driven. If ever any one died as a martyr, it was Mary Dyer, who was *legally murdered* on Boston Common, by the Magistrates of Massachusetts Bay, for the crime of worshipping God according to the dictates of her conscie nce. She ascended the scaffold firmly, calmly and with a holy serenity of countenance, as if the blessedness of a better world had already encircled her. And she died—sustained by a hope which it is feared her persecutors neverknew—the hope—the blessed assurance rather—of a welcome to the rest of the Lord.

"The Alchymist" by Miss S. J. Hale—good, very good. "Oriental Mysticism" by—no matter who—poor, very poor. "The Last Request" by B. B. Thacher is an admirable poem. We know not the author, but are inclined to think that the name appended to the poem is a fictitious one. Whoever he is—he is worthy of the praise.

We have thus gone over the Token for 1831. We have not noticed all the articles, for several of them--being neither particularly good, nor unconscionably bad, deserved nothing at our hands. We must confess that we have been unable to discover in the two American Annuals which we have received, very decided improvements above those of last year. There is a great deal of foolish writing in both—and so far as the poetry is concerned, we might cull from our newspapers—the frail and perishing things of a week's duration—better rhymes than those which fill the Souvenir and Token. But enough—we have done with Annuals—we would not review another for a cart-load of similar productions.

New England Weekly Review, Hartford, Oct. 25, 1830.

DEMONOLOGY AND WITCHCRAFT

(Scott)

This is the subject of the XII. volume of the Family Library—a valuable work now publishing in England. It is from the pen of Sir Walter Scott. The subject no doubt is well handled, although

66

we suspect Sir W. Scott is not exactly the man to reason coolly upon it. He has certainly given evidence in some of his writings of a slight bias of his mind to the marvellous and preternatural — in other words, he has a little of the old Highland superstition in his feelings.

Among the many cases of what is termed spectral illusion, Sir W. Scott mentions one, of an eminent lawyer who was attended by a physician from whom Sir Walter himself had the narrative. The patient was apparently sane in mind—his vigorous intellect had never been found subdued by the influence of imagination; and yet, with no symptoms of acute or alarming disease— with no real cause for melancholy in his worldly affairs, or in his own conscience, he was evidently the prey of some dark and secret grief, which was draining like the fabled vampyre, his very life blood. At length he yielded to the importunities of his physician, and disclosed the singular fact that he was dying, like D'Olivarez in the novel of Le Sage, because he was haunted by an apparation, to the actual existence of which he gave no credit, but that he was heart-broken and overcome by the imaginary presence of an abhorrent apparition. He stated that two or three years before he had been haunted for a considerable length of time by the apparition of a cat—which at last gave place to that of a gentleman usher, or waiting man which followed him in all directions, in his own house and that of others, invisible to all save himself. After a few months this too passed away, and was succeeded by a vision horrible to the sight, and painful to the imagination, being no other than the ghastly image of death itself—*the apparition of a skeleton.* We give the sequel of the story in the words of Sir Walter:

"The physician was distressed to perceive, from these details, how strongly this visionary apparition was fixed in the imagination of his patient. He ingeniously urged the sick man, who was then in bed, with questions concerning the circumstances of the phantom's appearance, trusting he might lead him, as a sensible man, into such contradictions and inconsistencies as might combat successfully the fantastic disorder which produced such fatal effects. 'This skeleton, then,' said the doctor, 'seems to you to be always present to your eyes?' 'It is my fate, unhappily,' answered the invalid, 'always to see it.' 'Then I understand,' continued the physician, 'it is now present to your imagination?' 'To my imagination it certainly is so,' replied the sick man. 'And in what part of the chamber do you now conceive the apparition to appear?' the physician inquired. 'Immediately at the foot of my bed; when the curtains are left a little open,' answered the invalid, 'the skeleton, to my thinking is placed between them, and fills the vacant space.' 'You say you are sensible of the delusion,' said his friend; 'have you firmness to convince yourself of the truth of this? Can you take courage eno ugh to rise and place yourself in the spot so seeming to be occupied, and convince yourself of the illusion?' The poor man sighed, and shook his head negatively. 'Well,' said the doctor, 'we will try the experiment otherwise.' Accordingly, he rose from his chair by the bedside, and placing himself between the two half-drawn curtains at the foot of the bed, indicated as the place occupied by the apparition, asked if the spectre was still visible? 'Not entirely so,' replied the patient, 'because your person is betwixt him and me; but I observe his skull peering above your shoulder.' It is alleged, the man of science started on the instant, despite philosophy, on receiving an answer ascertaining, with such minuteness, that the ideal spectre was close to his own person. He resorted to other means of investigation and cure, but with equally indifferent success. The patient sunk into deeper and deeper dejection, and died in the same distress of mind in which he had spent the latter months of his life; and his case remains a melancholy instance of the power of imagination to kill the body, even when its fantastic terrors cannot overcome the intellect of the unfortunate persons who suffer under them. The patient, in the present case, sunk under his malady; and the circumstances of his singular disorder remaining concealed, he did not, by his death and last illness, lose any of the well-merited reputation for prudence and sagacity which had attended him during the whole course of his life."

New England Weekly Review, Hartford, Nov. 15, 1830.

THE WATER WITCH

(Cooper)

This is the title of Cooper's new novel. We have read the work with some attention; and feel disposed to speak favorably of it. It is hardly to be compared to the Prairie, or the Last of the Mohicans, or even to the Pilot— but there are some scenes in it which are calculated to make the reader's blood thrill with excited feeling. The story is one of the "City of Gotham," in its olden times—amidst the Dutch, the negroes, and the buccaneers. The "Water Witch" is the name of a smuggling vessel, commanded by a strange, *outre* being who is known by the appellation of "Skimmer of the Seas." The heroine is a pretty Huguenot—"la belle Barbarie," and like all of Cooper's females is far from being so striking a personage as to fix the attention of the reader. The author in fact, fails miserably in his attempts to describe the lovely ones of Earth, and the finer and more delicate emotions of the heart. He is at home—perfectly so—in his delineations of natural scenery—in the turmoil and excitement of manly daring and professional hardihood—but he has little skill in metaphysical matters. He knows little of the human heart—its thousand delicate strings—swept over by as many impassioned feelings.

The passage of the Hell gate—the fight with the French vessel, and afterwards with the boats—the burning of the Coquette, and the miraculous escape upon the raft, are all fraught with deep and engrossing interest. It is in such descriptions that the secret of Cooper's popularity lies. There is little of startling and original thought in his writings. His style, for the most part is like his own 'Prairie' of the West—a uniform and unbroken level, luxuriant it may be, but wanting in the boldness and magnificence of a more diversified scenery.

New England Weekly Review, Hartford, Dec. 27, 1830.

MOORE'S BYRON, VOL. 2.

This volume is little calculated to induce a favorable opinion of the illustrious individual whose life and private writings it has laid open to public scrutiny. It is we fear pernicious—eminently so—in its tendency. The low licentiousness—the vulgarity, obscenity, and profanity, which distinguish his private correspondence should never have been cast thus profusely before the public. We would not for our right hand read this book before a sister—we would not shock the ears of aged piety by a revelation of its unpardonable and impious language. It is strange that Thomas Moore should have given such a volume to the world. It will be read indeed with interest—for it relates to one of the world's great spirits—but it will add no wreaths to the fame of its author; and it will only cast a deeper shadow upon the reputation of the illustrious dead. It will check the warm flow of that sympathy, which the melancholy strains of the poet, and the glorious death of the man, were so well calculated to call forth.

We admire—we almost worship, the sublimity of Byron's genius. He had a power which no other writer ever possessed—a lofty and overmastering intellect—a capability to grasp the dim and unfamiliar phantasies of mind and to mould them to his will—to call up from the unvisited depths of the human heart, feelings too terrible and too mighty for our nature. He passed by the better things of humanity—the calm of true philosophy—the holy consolations of religion—the kindly charities which "make existence sweet" and has drawn his bold characters from the darker passions of human nature. They are beings of misanthropy and power—endowed with a fearful capability of suffering, yet unhumbled by the rod of the chastener.—The moral tendency of such creations may well be questioned—but it is not of *them* that we complain. It is of the evident attempt on the part of Lord Byron to disseminate his poisonous principles—to shadow other bosoms with the doubt and misanthropy which darkened his own—to break down the distinctions between vice and virtue; and to extinguish in the hearts of his readers—the young, the innocent and the lovely—the pure and holy light of virtuous principles. In much of his writings it seems to have been his chief aim to portray virtue and moral grandeur in their loveliest and noblest manifestations—and then, to proclaim to the world that he had no faith in them—that he considered them as mockeries, that human affection had no enduring power—that its ties might be broken by a breath; and that the show of angelic virtues was but the covering of iniquity at heart. How often does he place the genuine language of pure and honorable love into the mouths of the vicious and unprincipled? Witness the letter from the *married* lover of Don Juan.

The private life of Lord Byron corresponded with his writings. Moore has exposed the dark errors and moral corruption of his friend, with the most unscrupulous fidelity. We are sorry for it—it was an unkind deed—and in our opinion, an unnecessary one. We would not willingly look upon such a picture of lofty genius and low depravity, as he has presented in the character of his illustrious subject.

Genius has too long been considered an apology for vice and hollow-heartedness. In our deliberate opinion it is only an aggravation of the offence. If the peculiar and unwonted endowments of Heaven—the rich gifts of intellect, which God has bestowed upon some of his favored creatures, are to be made the excuse of blaspheming the Giver, and violating his holy laws—we cannot hold our peace, and assent, even silently, to the abominable doctrine. Tell us not of the wayward propensities—the fierce, untamable passions which are the attendants of superior genius. Unless this doctrine is checked in the outset, we shall have hundreds of *would be geniuses* imitating Lord Byron, where they alone *can* imitate him, in the vices and follies which disgraced one of the noblest spirits of this, or any other age.

New England Weekly Review, Feb. 14, 1831.

A MODERN DISCOVERY

(Love Sickness)

'Tis said that the world is daily growing better—that intelligence and refinement are doing much for the improvement of our condi-

71

tion—that, in short, our ancestors were exceeding dunces, and that their favored progeny have an indisputable right to call them so. Ours is undoubtedly a glorious generation. We can boast of a thousand fine things which were never dreamed of by our grandfathers. Formerly a man's creed and Sunday dress were alike unchangeable. Now we change both like so many chameleons. Formerly it was considered a merit to be useful,—now, utility is a species of vulgarity incompatible with good society.—Whether these things, and a multitude of others of the same nature, furnish any decided evidence of improvement on the part of the generation which now is, we are not prepared to say. —Our individual opinion is, of course, of little consequence.

We find among other innovations upon long established matters, that the sentiments and notions of our ancestors upon the subject of love, and its operations upon the mental and physical nature of its possessor—sentiments which have been so long and so universally acknowledged—which have inspired the burning page of the poet and the thrilling delineations of the novelist,—are discarded as unworthy of our enlightened age. A late number of the Journal of Health, conducted by as merry a band of Physicians, as were those which initiated the Hypochondriac of Moliere into the mysteries of the Temple of Esculapius—ridicules the idea of a lady's pining away and dying "all for love," as an absuridity of the grossest kind. These same sapient disciples of Galen admit, of course, that a lady may fancy herself in love and even die with the idea still in her mind,—the verdict of all the maidenly ladies of her acquaintance may be that the poor creature came to her death of a broken heart—but the true cause of all, we are told, is, not an affection of the heart, but of the liver—not the wounding of the feathered shafts of Cupid, but the vice-like compression of steel and whalebone—not "Love's conversion of the heart's best blood to tears," but the lack of exercise and the atmosphere of the Ballroom.

Out upon these ungentlemanly Doctors! Is it not enough that they have prohibited the mazy dance and shut up the pleasant ball room,—that they have encased the delicate foot of beauty in vulgar *Caoutchouc*, making it a libel on the symmetry of the ancle, —that they have denounced the corset, even the corset, so dear to every lady of taste; and in the place of elegance and half-etherial beauty, associated with it deformity and disease? Must they, in addition to all this, quarrel with the beautiful imaginings of the heart and deny to the sentimental fair one the delightful and romantic idea of dying for love? Such an act of barbarity would be striking at the very root of poetry—the lopping away of the green branches of imagination, leaving only the naked and unseemly proportions of reality. What, no such commodities as broken hearts! No mental impalement upon Cupid's arrow like that of Giaour upon the spear of a Janizary!—No pining away in the solitude of blighted affection—no "concealment feeding like the worm i' the bud upon the damask cheek" of beauty! What then becomes of poetry and romance? Gone—"like the baseless fabric of a vision." Again we say, out upon these wielders of lancet and goosequill. They are the very Jack Cades of the sentimental world, and should be compelled, by universal decree, to lead a life of single blessedness,—to dine upon their own drugs and swallow their saddle-bags by way of desert.

In the days of our grandmothers every body knows that Court-ship and Love were serious affairs—business, which, once engaged in, was seldom or never given over until its "consumma-tion so devoutly to be wished"—a highway leading directly to honest Matrimony in which the traveller like Bunyan's Pilgrim pressed forward without turning to the right hand or the left. But ours is the age of flirtation, coquetry broken promises and

> "Vows which tremble on the lip but breathe not
> of the heart."

And now, these meddlesome Doctors are for taking away the only consolation of disappointed love—viz: the idea of pining away under the influence of the delectable and interesting malady of a broken heart:—and recommending to all who imagine themselves irrevocably in love to consult Halstead for the Dyspepsia or Beddoes for the liver complaint instead of sighing at the moonlight or weeping over a billet-doux.

New England Weekly Review, Hartford, April 4, 1831.

JOHN TRUMBULL

This distinguished son of Connecticut died at Detroit on the 11th inst. aged 81. He was born at Watertown, in the parish of Westbury, on the 24th of April, 1750. He received his education at Yale College. In 1771, he was chosen one of the tutors of the Institution. In 1773, he was admitted to the bar in Connecticut, and afterwards continued his studies in the office of John Adams at Boston. Previous to this, he had written his "Progress of Dulness,"—a satirical poem—and in 1775 the first part of his celebrated "M'Fingal" made its appearance. In 1789 he was appointed Attorney to the State for Hartford County. The city of Hartford he has frequently represented in the Legislature. In 1801 he was appointed a Judge of the Superior Court, and in 1808 Judge of the Supreme Court of Errors, which offices he held until 1819. In 1820 a collection of his poems was published in two volumes. He left this city in 1825, and fixed his residence at Detroit, in the family of his daughter.

We have never personally known Judge Trumbull—but there are those around us who will long love and cherish his memory. His learning--his brilliant powers of conversation—his keen wit—and his high poetical genius, have endeared him to all who knew him, and could appreciate his splendid gifts of intellect. His M'Fingal is, beyond comparison, the most popular poem ever produced by an American writer. Its satire, keen and terrible—its ready sense of the truly ridiculous—its unrivalled humour—its classical embellishments—its odd associations—its easy versification, and its earnest patriotism, will render it an object of interest to the scholar and the patriot, long after a score of our modern popular writers shall have passed away, and their works shall have followed them, into forgetfulness.

Peace to the memory of the patriotic old man!—He died in the "far West,"—away from his own loved Connecticut, and the scenes of his childhood, his love, his ambition. His grave was made by the hand of strangers. But to that grave shall the gifted and high-hearted of our land go up in coming years, while

"After life's fitful fever he sleeps well."

New England Weekly Review, Hartford, May 30, 1831.

THE LITERARY REMAINS OF
JOHN G. C. BRAINARD

Introduction

There is a feeling of reverence associated with our reminiscences of departed worth and genius. It is too holy and deep for
outward manifestation. It hovers closely around the heart, sweeping in secret the fine and hidden chords of our better sympathies.
In contemplating the character of the subject of this sketch, I
feel in no ordinary degree, the peculiar delicacy of the task I have
undertaken. It is like lifting the shroud from the still face of the
dead, that the living may admire its yet lingering loveliness. I
almost feel as if I were writing in the presence of the disembodied
spirit of the departed;—as if the eye of his modest and unpretending genius were following the pen, which traces his brief history.

John Gardiner Calkins Brainard, was born at New London,
Connecticut, in October, 1796. He was the son of the late Hon.
Jeremiah G. Brainard, formerly a Judge of the Superior Court in
that State. His preparatory studies were under the direction of
his elder brother, who is at this time a highly respectable member of the Connecticut bar. He entered Yale College at the age
of fifteen;—and soon gave evidence of the possession of a superior gift of intellect. His genius was not of that startling nature,
which blazes out suddenly from the chaos of an unformed character, dazzling with its unexpected brilliance. It developed itself
gradually and quietly. It was perceptible to others even before
its possessor seemed conscious of its influence. Never intrusive,
and always shrinking from competition, it called forth an admiration which had no alloy of envy. There was a modesty in the
manifestations of his genius,—a disinterestedness, at times
almost approaching carelessness, which forbade the suspicion of
rivalship, and which discovered no inclination to contend for
those honors which all felt were within his grasp.

During his residence at Yale College he was a universal
favorite. Although, even at that early period, something of the

sadness which clouded his after life occasionally gathered around him, he had all the cheerfulness of a happy child in the society of his friends. His smile was ever ready to greet their good humored sallies; and he had, in turn, his own peculiar faculty of awaking mirthful and pleasant emotions. In his gayer moments of social intercourse, the drollery of his manner—the singularity in the mode of his expression, and in the association of his ideas,—something of which is perceptible in his lighter poems,—rendered his society peculiarly fascinating. His wit seldom took a personal direction. It played lightly over the easy current of his conversation,—brilliant—sparkling—but perfectly harmless.

He was not a hard student. He wanted in a great degree even the common stimulus of Ambition. He had no desire to triumph over his fellows. He was contented with his own retirement of thought. His purposes of life, too, were shadowy, undefined and mutable. He had consequently, no given point upon which to direct the powers of his mind. The rays were scattered carelessly abroad, which should have been concentrated upon one bright and burning focus.

On leaving College, he returned to New London, and entered the office of his brother William F. Brainard Esq. as a Student at Law. While in this situation, he experienced a disappointment of that peculiar nature, which so often leaves an indelible impression upon the human heart. It probably had some influence upon the tenor of his after life. It threw a cloud between him and the sunshine;—it turned back upon its fountain a frozen current of rebuked affections. This circumstance has been mentioned only as affording in some measure, a solution of what might have been otherwise inexplicable in the depression of his maturer years. Perhaps there are few men of sensitive feelings and high capacities with whom something of the kind does not exist,—something which the heart reverts to with mingled tenderness and sorrow, —one master chord of feeling the tones of whose vibrations are loudest and longest,—one strong hue in the picture of existence, which blends with, and perchance overpowers all others,—one passionate remembrance, which, at times, like the rod of the Levite swallows up all other emotions. This great passion of the heart, when connected with disappointed feeling, is not easily forgotten. Mirth, wine, the excitement of convivial intercourse, —the gaities of fashion,—the struggles of ambition, may produce a temporary release from its presence. But a word carelessly uttered—a flower—a tone of music—a strain of poetry,—"Striking the electric chain wherewith we are darkly bound," may recall it again before the eye of the mind,—and the memory of the past— the glow and ardor of passion—the hope—the fear—the disappoint- ment—will crowd in upon the heart. It is at such moments that the image of old happiness rises up like the Astarte of Manfred, only to mock the sick senses with an ungratifying visitation.

After his admission to the Bar he removed to the City of Middletown, in the year 1819, and commenced the practice of his profession. His situation was by no means congenial to his feelings. He had grown weary of the dull routine of his studies. To use his own language, "he was of a temperament much too sensitive for his own comfort in a calling, which exposed him to personal altercation, contradiction, and that sharp and harsh collision, which tries and strengthens the passions of the heart, at least as much as it does the faculties of the mind."

Sensitive to a fault,—with scarcely a desire for distinction in the profession which had been assigned him, with no feeling of avarice, and with little of worldly prudence, he yielded to the lassitude and unnerving relaxation of mind and body to which every young professional man is exposed, while waiting for the tardy manifestations of public favor. Too much is often expected of a mind like that of Brainard. The world judges from external appearance; and is ever ready to condemn as eccentric and un- profitable, the bias of that genius, which from its very nature is unable to follow in the vulgar path of common and plodding intellect. Locke, whose metaphysical discoveries are equalled only by those of Newton in the material universe, was accounted unfit even for a physician. Akenside lived unrespected in his native town, and his poetical reputation was injurious to his profession. Blackstone and Lord Mansfield bade farewell to the muses when they betook themselves seriously to the law. Darwin prudently concealed his poetry, until his medical reputation was established. Home published Douglass, and lost for so doing the pastoral care of his parish. Sir Richard Blackmore enjoyed an almost unparalleled reputation as a physician: He published his

77

poetry, and there were "none to do him reverence."

Genius has its own peculiar path. It cannot float upon the common current of the world. It has its own ideal dwelling-place—its unparticipated joys; and its "heart knoweth its own bitterness, neither does the stranger intermeddle therewith." Standing aloof from the common path,—an alien in feeling and action,—its possessor has been too often regarded in conformity with the counsel of the dying man in Otway's tragedy:

> . . . ."Shun
> The man that's singular. His mind's unsound--
> His spleen o'erweighs his brain."

The apparent listlessness and inactivity of Brainard were productive of no little disappointment and anxiety on the part of his friends. They saw him turning away from the struggles of business, and the path of ambition, apparently regardless of what Roger Williams has quaintly termed, "the Worlde's great Trinitie," Pleasure, Profit and Honor;—and while they acknowledged his high intellectual capacities, they lamented his want of worldly wisdom.

During his residence in Middletown he composed some of his minor poems;—and made several contributions to a literary paper in the City of New Haven, conducted by the late Cornelius Tuthill, Esq. While here, he made no effort to win the attention of the public. His door was always open to the lounger; and his numerous friends and associates were never unwelcome, except when they visited him in the character of clients.

Weary of his experience of the profession for which he had been educated, he turned at last to the only path which seemed open to him; and entered upon the uncertain and precarious destiny of a literary writer. He had found himself unable to mingle in the hot and eager strife of that political arena, which the institutions and spirit of our country have thrown open to numberless competitors; and for which the profession of law is peculiarly adapted. To bear off the political palm,—to stamp upon passing events the impress of a master mind,—to trample down the weak and wrestle with the strong, required nerves of "sterner stuff" than those of Brainard. A stranger to malevolence and party bitterness himself,

he shrank from a collision with the ruder and turbulent spirits of
political ambition. It would be well for our country, if her party
contests were always of such a character, that the sensitive and
the ingenuous, the pure-hearted and the gifted might minister at
her political altars, without soiling the white ephod of their
priesthood by a contact with treachery, corruption and violence.

In February, 1822, he entered upon the duties of an Editor in
the City of Hartford, having contracted for conducting the Connecticut Mirror, with its publisher, Mr. P. B. Goodsell. Unknown at
this time, to fame, and struggling with a gathering despondency,
he began his literary career. His anticipations were by no means
those of buoyant and elastic feeling. His hope was like that
described by Cowley:—

"Whose weak being ruined is
Alike if it succeed and if it miss,
Whom good or ill doth equally confound,
And both the horn's of fate's dilemma wound."

He had failed in the profession to which he had devoted the morning of his existence. He was making an experiment, upon the
issue of which the character of his future destiny depended. He
had seen enough of life—he had felt enough of the workings of
his own spirit, to know that his "thoughts were not the thoughts
of other men,"—that a gulf, wider than that which yawned between
Dives and the beatified spirits of happiness, separated him from
the common sympathies of the busy, grasping, unnatural world.
He went to his weekly task as to the performance of an unwelcome duty,—but without physical energy or firmness of purpose.
His temperament was totally unfitted for the rough collisions of
editorial controversy. There was too much gentleness in his
nature,—too much charity for the offending, and too much modesty
in his own pretensions, to allow of any rudeness of criticism or
severity of censure. His writings in the Connecticut Mirror are
uniformly gentlemanly and goodnatured. It is impossible to discover in them any thing like malice or wantonness of satire. He
was the first to award due praise to his literary brethren. His
criticisms were those of a man willing to lend his fine ear to the
harmonies of poetry, and his clear healthful eye to the light of

intellectual beauty, wherever these were to be seen or heard. In deciding upon the merits of a new publication, he did not pause to inquire who was the author, or coldly weigh in the balance of his selfishness, the probable effect upon himself, of a favorable or unfavorable expression of opinion. He had nothing of that carping, mole-visioned spirit of criticism, which has neither eye to see, nor heart to appreciate truth and beauty in others; but which like the torch, which the ancients ascribed to their personification of Malevolence, lingers only upon faults.

The originality and spirit of his poetical writings soon attracted attention. His pieces were extensively copied, and, not unfrequently, with high encomium. The voice of praise is always sweet, but doubly so when it falls for the first time upon a youthful ear. But, Brainard was one of those who "bear their faculties meekly." Although publishing, week after week, poems which would have done honor to the genius of Burns and Wordsworth, he never publicly betrayed any symptoms of vanity. He held on the quiet and even tenor of his way, apparently regardless of that prodigality of intellectual beauty which blossomed around him. With but a moiety of his powers, more ardent and aspiring spirits would have striven mightily for the sunshine of applause. Brainard sought the shade. The fine current of his mind, like the 'sacred river' of the Kubla Khan, "meandered with an easy (*sic*) motion." in the silence and the coolness of abstracted thought, far below the noisy and heated atmosphere of the world. Its music was for himself alone. He cared not that the great world should hear it. It was like that hidden brooklet which Coleridge speaks of,—

.... "To the sleeping woods all night
Singing a quiet tune" ....

a stream, it is true, which burst forth occasionally into the live sunshine, like the flow of molten diamonds, but which seemed to murmur sweeter, where it caught its glimpses of blue sky and sailing cloud, through the dim vistas of the shaded solitude.

Aside from its original poetry and occasional notices of new books, the Mirror, while under his control hardly rose to mediocrity. The editorial remarks were usually comprised in a few short and hastily written paragraphs. There was a childish playfulness in his brief notices of important events. His political speculations were puerile and boyish. He turned off the Tariff with a humorous comparison or a quaint quotation; and dismissed the subject of the Presidency with a jeu de esprit. Feeling himself unqualified by education or habit for the discussion of these matters, he would not for the enjoyment of a fictitious reputation,

> .... "Get him glass eyes,
> And like a scurvy politician seem
> To see the things he did not."

He received considerable assistance from his brother,—whose frequent communications are marked by strong, nervous and original thought.

His habits of self reliance, of a gentle retirement into the calm beauty of his own mind rendered him, in a measure indifferent to the opinion of the world. Yet he loved society—the society of the gifted and intellectual—and of those who had become accustomed to his peculiarities of manner and feeling, who could appreciate his merit, or relish his good natured jests and "mocks and knaveries," and laugh with him at what he considered the ludicrous eagerness of the multitude after the vanities of existence. In larger and mixed circles his peculiar sensitiveness was a frequent cause of unhappiness. Amidst his gaiety and humour, a word spoken inadvertently—some unmeaning gesture—some casual inattention or unlucky oversight, checked at once, the free glow of his sprightly conversation—the jest died upon his lip,—and the melancholy which had been lifted from his heart, fell back again with increased heaviness.

A writer in one of our Daily Journals,* in a brief but very eloquent notice of the death of Brainard, thus speaks of his intellectual character while a resident in Hartford: "Brainard did not make much show in the world. He was an unassuming and unambitious man—but he had talents which should have made him our pride. They were not showy or dazzling—and perhaps that is the reason that the general eye did not rest upon him—but he had a keen discriminating susceptibility, and a taste exquisitely re-

Boston Statesman of 1828. (Whittier's note).

fined and true."...."Brainard had no enemies. It was not that his character was negative or his courtesy universal. There was a directness in his manner, and a plain-spoken earnestness in his address, which could never have been wanting in proper discrimination. He would never have compromised with the unworthy for their good opinion. But it was his truth--his fine, open, ingenuous truth--bound up with a character of great purity and benevolence, which won love for him. I never met a man of whom all men spoke so well. I fear I never shall. When I was introduced to him, he took me aside and talked with me for an hour. I shall never forget that conversation. He made no common-place remarks. He would not talk of himself, though I tried to lead him to it. He took a high intellectual tone, and I never have heard its beauty or originality equalled. He knew wonderfully well the secrets of mental relish and development; and had evidently examined himself till he had grown fond, as every one must who does it, of a quiet, contemplative, self-cultivating life. He had gone on with this process until the spiritual predominated entirely over the material man. He was all soul--all intellect--and he neglected therefore, the exciting ambitions and the common habits which keep the springs of ordinary life excited and healthy--and so he died--and I know not that for his own sake we should mourn."

The citizens of Hartford were by no means unmindful of the real worth of Brainard, and if anything of an unpleasant nature occurred in his intercourse with them, it might generally be traced to his own susceptibility and tenderness of feeling. The writer from whom I have just quoted, thus describes the circumstances under which he first saw the subject of his sketch: "The first time I ever saw him, I met him in a gay and fashionable circle. He was pointed out to me as the poet Brainard--a plain, ordinary looking individual, careless in his dress, and apparently without the least outward claim to the attention of those who value such advantages, but there was no person there so much or so flatteringly attended to. He was among those who saw him every day and knew him familiarly; and I almost envied him, as he went round, the unqualified kindness and even affection, with which every bright girl and every mother in that room received him. He was evidently the idol, not only of the poetry-loving and gentler sex--but also of the young men who were about him--an evidence of worth, let me say, which is as high as it is uncommon."

In 1824-25, he prepared for the press a small volume of his poems. It was published at New York in the Spring of 1825. It contains about 40 short pieces of poetry, most of which were cut from the files of the Mirror with little or no revision. The quaint humor of the author appears in the title page: "Occasional Pieces of Poetry, by John G.C. Brainard.

Some said, "John, print it;" others said, "Not so;"—
Some said, "It might do good;" others said, "No."
                                            Bunyan's Apology

The introduction is brief and characteristic: "The author of the following pieces has been induced to publish them in a book, from considerations which cannot be interesting to the public. Many of these little poems have been printed in the *Connecticut Mirror;* and the others are just fit to keep them company. No apologies are made, and no criticisms deprecated. The common place story of the importunities of friends, though it had its share in the publication, is not insisted upon; but the vanity of the author, if others choose to call it such, is a natural motive; and the hope of "making a little something by it," is an honest acknowledgement, if it is a poor excuse."

In this humble and unpretending manner, a volume was introduced to the public, of which it is not too much to say, that it contains more pure, beautiful poetry, than any equal number of pages ever published in this country. I would make no rash assertion. Fame cannot visit Brainard in his grave—and I would not wrong his memory by exaggerated eulogium. Nor would I detract in the slightest degree from the just reputation of the living.* As an American I am proud of the many gifted spirits who have laid their offerings upon the altar of our national literature. I believe them capable of greater and more successful efforts. I would encourage them onward. There is a growing disposition at home and abroad to reward literary exertion. And even if such were not the fact, is there nothing in the mild process of intellectual refinement, which is of itself worth more than the great world can bestow? "Poetry" says Coleridge, "has been to me its own exceeding great reward." This consciousness of

*Compare the remainder of the paragraph with "American Writers," p. 106.

rightly improving the endowments of Heaven,—of possessing a pure, internal fountain of innocent happiness, to which the spirit may turn for its refreshing from the fever of the world,—this contented self reliance,

> "Which nothing earthly gives, or can destroy,
> The soul's calm sunshine and the heartfelt joy"

is far more to be desired than the deceitful murmurs of applause falling upon the craving ear of an unsatisfied spirit. Goethe learned this truth, long before the public eye was fixed upon him. He could be happy and satisfied in the enjoyment of his own intellectual paradise, even before the world had realized or acknowledged its exceeding beauty. In such a state the mind becomes worthy of its origin. It realizes in Time, something of its expansion in Eternity.

It is not to be denied that some of the poems in this little collection were totally unworthy of Brainard's genius,—hasty, careless, and even in some instances below mediocrity—serving only as a foil to the exceeding beauty of the others. But what poet of modern days has ever published a perfect volume?— Byron threw his hasty, but powerful productions before the public with beauty wedded to deformity. Southey "discourses fustian" in his Joan of Arc; and in the midst of his wild dream of Eastern wonder tells his ridiculous story of Kehama's ride into Hell over nine several bridges. Wordsworth, with all his fine perceptions of natural beauty, and his exquisite philosophy, sinks at times into the most disgusting puerility,—the pathos and sentiment of an overgrown baby. Even the gifted Shelley wearies us with his sickly conceits and unsubstantial theories;—and the author of St. Agnes Eve is mawkish and affected in his Endymion. It is certainly creditable to our Literary Reviews and Journals that, notwithstanding its obvious defects, the volume of Brainard was received with general and liberal encomium. The North American Review—one of our ablest periodicals—in a notice, generally favorable and extending through several pages, after speaking of the propensity of American writers to indulge in an unnatural and affected style—"the contortions of the Sybil, without the inspiration:"—makes the following remarks upon the particular subject in question:—"The instances are rare in which the charge of affectation can be made against Mr. Brainard, whatever may be his faults of taste and execution; or in which his practice can be said to sanction the doctrine that

"One line for sense and one for rhyme
Is quite enough at any time."

He seldom aims at more than he can accomplish: the chief misfortune with him is, that he should be contented sometimes to accomplish so little, and that little in so imperfect a manner. That he possesses much of the genuine spirit and power of poetry, no one can doubt who reads some of the pieces in this volume, yet there are others which, if not absolutely below mediocrity, would never be suspected as coming from a soil watered by the dews of Castaly. They might pass off very well as exercises in rhyme of an incipient poet, the first efforts of pluming the wing for a bolder flight, and they might hold for a day an honorable place in the corner of a gazette, but to a higher service, a more conspicuous station, they could not wisely be called. In short, if we take all the author's compositions in this volume together, nothing is more remarkable concerning them than their inequality; the high poetical beauty and strength, both in thought and language of some parts, and the want of good taste and the extreme negligence of others."

Although the success which attended his first publication was such as might have stimulated one of a different temperament to greater and more systematic exertion, it had no sensible effect on Brainard. His friends urged him to undertake a poem of some length in which he could concentrate the full vigor and beauty of his poetical powers; but he could never be prevailed upon to task his mind with the effort. He continued however to publish at long intervals, his "occasional pieces." These are now collected for the first time in the present volume.

It is very probable that lassitude and bodily debility may have been the prominent cause of the inactivity of Brainard even after the general voice had pronounced him capable of "marking the age with his name." Fame may "minister to a mind diseased;" but it cannot re-fill the exhausted fountains of existence; and that for which health and happiness have been sacrificed; may prove

85

at last a mockery—like "delicates poured upon the mouth shut up, or as meats set upon a grave."

In the Spring of 1827, his health, which had for some time been failing, admonished him to seek its restoration by means of a temporary release from the duties of his profession. He returned to the quiet of his birthplace. There, all was affection and sympathy; and for these his sick spirit had longed "even as the servant earnestly desireth the shadow." His illness soon assumed the fearful character of a decided consumption.

During the Summer he spent a short time on Long Island. While here he composed that beautiful and touching sketch "The Invalid on the East end of Long Island," which cannot but be admired for its touching pathos, and exquisite description. It is remarkable as the only piece in which his sickness is alluded to. He did not wish to turn the public eye upon himself. He was contented with the sympathy and affectionate kindness of his intimate friends. In the loneliness of his sick chamber these were worth more to him than the plaudits of a world.

He never returned to Hartford. The slow but certain progress of disease compelled him to resign into other hands the editorial department of his paper. Notwithstanding the circumstances under which it was written, his brief and pertinent valedictory, is buoyant with the author's characteristic cheerfulness.

He wrote while at New London, several short poems which were published in the Mirror. These bear no evidence of that depression which so generally accompanies a lingering illness. They are fanciful and brilliant—indicating a clear and healthful mental vision, unaffected by the circumstance of physical decay.

To most minds there is something terrible in the steady and awful decline of the powers of nature,—the gradual loosening of the silver cord of existence. It is in truth a fearful thing to perish slowly in the very spring of existence,—to feel day after day, our hold on life less certain,—to look out upon Nature with an eye and a spirit capable of realizing its beauty, and yet to feel that to us it is forbidden, —to be conscious of deep affections and tender sympathies and yet to know that these must perish in our own bosoms, unshared and solitary,—to feel the fever of ambition, without the power to satisfy its thirst,—and, ourselves dark and despairing, to "look into happiness through the eyes of others." But Brainard was happy in the hour of sickness and the failing of his strength. Death for him had few terrors.—Young as he was he had learned to turn aside from the world,—to live in it without leaning upon it. His were the consolations of that religion whose inheritance is not of this world. While in health--in the widest range of his fancy—in the purest play of his humor, he had never indulged in irreverence or profanity, for there was always a deep under-current of religious feeling, tempering the lighter elements of his disposition. He had moreover made himself thoroughly acquainted with the great truths of Christianity by a long and careful study of the sacred volume. And when, to use his own language, he turned

> "Away from all that's bright and beautiful—
> To the sick pillow and the feverish bed,"

the pure and sustaining influence of that peace which is "not such as the world giveth" was around him, "like the shadow of a great rock in a weary land." There is a refining process in sickness. The human spirit is purified and made better by the ordeal of affliction. The perishing body is strongly contrasted with its living guest—the one sinking into ruins—the other 'secure in its existence,' and strong in its imperishable essence. It may be that, according to the poet,

> "The soul's dark cottage, battered and decayed,
> Still lets in light through chinks which Time has made,"

and that when the pleasures and varieties of the world are stealing away forever—when the frail foothold of existence is washing rapidly away—like the disciple of the Egyptian Priesthood, who, in ascending the mystic ladder of the temple of Isis, was compelled to grasp the round above him, while the one beneath him was crumbling in pieces—the human spirit is led upward by the very insufficiency of its earthly support, until at last it takes hold on Heaven. In the hour of health and high enjoyment, a thousand images of earthly beauty rise between us and the better land. It is only when those "which look out at the window are darkened" that the full glory of the beatific vision is realized.

It is in the shadow, and not in the bright sunshine that the eye looks farthest into the blue mysteries above us.

The Rev. Mr. M'Ewen pastor of the Church of which Brainard was a member, in a letter to the Rev. Dr. Hawes of Hartford, thus describes the last hours of his friend. "In my first visit to him, two or three months before his death, he said:—'I am sick and near death, and I ought not to be too confident how I should act or feel had I a prospect of health and the worldly pleasures and prosperity which it would offer. But, if I know myself I would were I well, devote my life to the service of Jesus Christ.' I stated some of the main doctrines of Christianity. 'These are scripture,' he said —'they are true, and delightful to me. The plan of Salvation in the Gospel is all that I wish for;—it fills me with wonder and gratitude; and makes the prospect of death not only peaceful but joyful.—'My salvation,' he continued, 'is not to be effected by a profession of religion; but when I read Christ's requirements, and look round on my friends and acquaintance, I cannot be content without performing this public duty.' He was propounded, and in due time, pale and feeble, yet manifestly with mental joy and serenity, he came to the house of God, professed his faith and was baptized, and entered into covenant with God and his people. The next Sabbath the Lord's Supper was administered. It was wet and he could not be out. His disappointment was great. A few friends went to his room and communed with him there in this ordinance. While his father's family and others, during the scene, were dissolved in tears, he sat with dignity and composure, absorbed in the interesting ceremony in which he was engaged. In my last interview with him, after he was, at his request, left alone with me, he said: 'I wish not to be deceived about my state—but I am not in the usual condition to try myself. No one abuses a sick man—every thing around me is sympathy and kindness. I used to be angry when people spoke what was true of me. I have now no resentment. I can forgive all, and pray I think for the salvation of all. I am not tried with pain. I have hardly any outward trial.' 'But,' said I, 'you have one great trial—you must soon part with life:' 'And I am willing' he replied. 'The Gospel makes my prospect delightful. God is a God of truth, and I think I am reconciled to him.' I saw him no more, but was told that he died in peace."

He died September 26th, 1828. The event was widely deplored.
The poetry of Brainard had addressed itself directly to the heart,
and had made its author beloved by thousands who had never
seen him. Brainard has beautifully described the sorrows of the
Tuscan philosopher when his favorite Pleiad had vanished from
its clustering sisterhood. It was with something of this feeling
that the friends of American genius looked out upon and numbered
the lights of our literary horizon, and mourned for that missing
star, whose rising was so full of promise. In the places of his
former residence the news of his death, though long expected,
came like a sudden and mournful visitation. All felt, more sensibly
than ever, the true worth of the noble spirit which had been among
them. In his own family there was that deeper "grief which
passeth show"—a sorrow which could be alleviated only by the
consolations of that hope which sustained in his last moments,
their departed relative.

"Where shall they turn to mourn him less?—
When cease to hear his cherished name?
Time cannot teach Forgetfulness,
When Grief's full heart is fed by fame."

The person of Brainard was rather below the ordinary standard—
a circumstance which gave him a great deal of uneasiness, and
any allusion to it, however playful, never failed to injure deeply
his sensitive feelings. His features were expressive of mildness
and reflection. There was a dreamy listlessness in his eye,
which, however, gave way to the changes of feeling and passion.
I cannot forbear introducing in this place an extract of a letter
from a Lady, highly distinguished in the walks of Literature,—
one who knew Brainard well, and who has on another occasion,
paid a beautiful and just tribute to his memory:
"To the intellectual power, and poetical eminence of Mr.
Brainard, the public will undoubtedly do justice. But those who
knew and valued him as a *friend*, can bear testimony to the intrinsic excellencies of his character. They were admitted with
a generous freedom into the sanctuary of his soul, and saw those
fountains of deep and disinterested feeling which were hidden
from casual observation. Friendship was not in him a modifica-

tion of selfishness, lightly conceived, and as lightly dissolved. His sentiments respecting it, were formed on the noble models of ancient story,—and he proved himself capable of its delicate perceptions, and its undeviating integrities. His heart had an aptitude both for its confidential interchange, and its sacred responsibilities. In his intercourse with society, he exhibited neither the pride of genius, nor the pedantry of knowledge. To the critick he might have appeared deficient in personal dignity. So humbly did he think of himself, and his own attainments, that the voice of approbation and kindness, seemed necessary to assure his spirits, and even to sustain his perseverance in the labours of literature.—Possessed both of genuine wit, and of that playful humour which rendered his company sought and admired, he never trifled with the feelings of others, or aimed to shine at their expense. Hence he expected the same regard to his own mental comfort—and was exceedingly vulnerable to the careless jest, or to the chillness of reserve.

"It did not require the eye of intimacy to discover that he was endowed with an acute sensibility. This received early nurture, and example in the bosom of most affectionate relatives. The endearing associations connected with his paternal mansion, preserved their freshness and force, long after he ceased to be an inmate there. It was ever a remedy for his despondency to elicit from him descriptions of the scenery of his native place, of the rambles of his boyhood, of the little boat in which he first dared the waves;—but more especially of his beloved parents,—of his aged grandmother,—and of those fraternal sympathies which constituted so great a part of his happiness. When he had been for years a denizen of the busy world, and had mingled in those competitions which are wont to wear the edge from the finer feelings, a visit to his *home,* was an unchanged subject of joyous anticipation, of cherished recollection. At one of his last departures from that dear spot, previous to his return thither *to die;*—he stood upon the deck of the boat, watching each receding vestige of spire, tree, roof and billow, with a lingering and intense affection. Perceiving himself to be observed, he dashed away the large tears that were gathering like rain-drops, and conquering his emotion, said in a careless tone,—"Well, they are good folks there at home,—*all good but me;* that was the reason they sent me away." –The efforts which he continually put forth during his intercourse with mankind, to conceal his extreme susceptibility, sometimes gave to his manners the semblance of levity. Hence he was liable to misconstruction, and a consciousness of this, by inducing occasional melancholy and seclusion, threw him still further from these sympathies for which his affectionate spirit languished. Still it cannot be said that his sensibility had had a morbid tendency. It shrank indeed, like the Mimosa, but it had no worm at its root. Its gushings forth, were in admiration of the charms of nature,–and in benevolence to the humblest creature,–to the poor child in the street, and to the forest-bird. It had affinity with love to God, and with good-will to man. Had his life been prolonged, and he permitted to encircle with the beautiful domestick charities a household hearth of his own, the true excellencies of his heart would have gained more perfect illustration. It possessed a simplicity of trusting confidence,– a fullness of tender and enduring affection which would there have found free scope, and legitimate action. There he might have worn as a crown, that exquisite sensibility, which among proud and lofty spirits he covered as a blemish,–or shrank from as a reproach. But it pleased the Almighty early to transfer him, where loneliness can no longer settle as a cloud over his soul,– nor the coarse enginery which earth employs jar against its harp-strings, and obstruct its melody."

The poetry, which Brainard has left behind him, should be considered only in the light of a beautiful promise,–an earnest of the capabilities of a mind untasked by severe discipline, and almost unconscious of its own power. His productions were all hasty and unstudied, given to the press without revision—without a signature, and with nothing but their intrinsic worth to recommend them to public favor. Much allowance should be made for the circumstances under which they were written. Whoever has had an experimental knowledge of the editorial life, will acknowledge the extreme difficulty of giving uniform polish and beauty to the original columns of a newspaper. The mind revolts at the idea of a weekly task,–a defined and steadily exacted labor of intellect. In the intellectual temperament of genius there are seasons of listlessness and inactivity—when the bent bow relaxes from its tension—when in the language of Sterne, "the thoughts rise heavy and pass gummous through the pen." To write at such times for the edification or amusement of others is, at least, a painful and unnatural effort. It is like exacting responses from the Pythoness when deprived of her tripod.

Yet, notwithstanding the difficulties and disadvantages under which most of the poems in this volume were written—unpolished and unconnected as they are, by the mind which conceived them, they are such as would do honor to "longer scrolls and loftier lyres." They have certainly the qualities of genuine poetry. Study and revision might have polished and developed more fully their native colorings, but could have added little to their intrinsic excellence.

The longest poem in this collection is the Address to Connecticut River. It is a specimen of beautiful description. Its versification is easy and flowing, without the chiming monotony of the old school writers in their use of the same measure. The thoughts are perfectly natural. The images pass before us like old and familiar friends. We have seen and known them all before: not in books, but in the great open volume of nature. The paragraph commencing,

> "And there are glossy curls and sunny eyes,
> As brightly lit, and bluer than thy skies."

is a splendid picture: the master's hand is distinctly visible. There is nothing dim, or shadowy or meagre in its outlines,—it is the pencilling of a Leonardo de Vinci, full of life and vigor and beauty.

There is much of the true spirit of the old English Ballads in the Black Fox, Matchit Moodus, the Shad Spirit, and other poems of this description. His graver poems are, however more worthy of eulogium, although from the majority of his readers they may have met with a less cordial reception. But in truth the mind tires of continual solemnity and gloom—and it is perhaps better to laugh occasionally over the designs of Hogarth than to sup full of horrors with Salvator Rosa. Brainard's humor is, in fact, the mere sportiveness of innocence.

There is one important merit in his poetry which would redeem a thousand faults. It is wholly American. If he "babbles o' green fields" and trees they are such as of right belong to us. He does not talk of the palms and cypress where he should describe the rough oak and sombre hemlock. He prefers the lowliest blossom of Yankee-land to the gorgeous magnolia and the orange bower of another clime. It is this which has made his poetry popular and his name dear in New-England.

It has been often said that the New World is deficient in the elements of poetry and romance;* that its bards must of necessity linger over the classic ruins of other lands; and draw their sketches of character from foreign sources, and paint Nature under the soft beauty of an Eastern sky. On the contrary, New England is full of Romance; and her writers would do well to follow the example of Brainard. The great forest which our fathers penetrated—the red men—their struggle and their disappearance—the Powwow and the War-dance—the savage inroad and the English sally—the tale of superstition, and the scenes of Witchcraft,—all these are rich materials of poetry. We have indeed no classic vale of Tempe—no haunted Parnassus—no temple, gray with years, and hallowed by the gorgeous pageantry of idol worship—no towers and castles over whose moonlight ruins gathers the green pall of the ivy. But we have mountains pillowing a sky as blue as that which bends over classic Olympus; streams as bright and beautiful as those of Greece or Italy,— and forests richer and nobler than those which of old were haunted by Sylph and Dryad.

The moral tone of the poems in this collection is certainly deserving of high commendation, in an age, which has been poisoned by the licentiousness of poetry,—by the school of Moore and Byron and Shelley,—to say nothing of their thousand imitators.

There would seem to be a strong temptation attending the process of poetical composition to give imagination the legitimate place of truth: to make boldness and originality the primary objects at the expense of virtuous sentiment and religious feeling. But who that peruses the Poems of Brainard will charge him with having obeyed this general tendency. Playfulness and humor they may indeed find,—but no irreverence; no licentious description- no daring revolt of the dust and ashes of humanity against the wisdom and power of the Creator.

* Compare this paragraph with "American Romance," p. 106.

There is a deep religious feeling evinced in the lines commencing: "All sights are fair to the recovered blind." —The last stanza seems to breathe the melodious murmurs of the harp of Zion:

'Tis somewhat like the burst from death to life;
   From the grave's cerements to the robes of Heaven;
From sin's dominion, and from passion's strife
   To the pure freedom of a soul forgiven;
When all the bonds of death and hell are riven,
And mortals put on immortality;
   When fear, and care, and grief away are driven,
And Mercy's hand has turned the golden key,
   And Mercy's voice has said, "Rejoice--thy soul is free!"

(Summer, 1832)

''THE NERVOUS MAN''

Messrs. Editors: The enclosed MSS. are the literary remains of an esteemed friend of mine, who a short time since kneaded himself to death for the Dyspepsia, agreeably to the prescriptions of Dr. Halsted.

My friend made no pretensions to genius. He was a hard student, but the world has been little wiser for it. His literary appetite, like his physical, exceeded his digestion. He always seemed to me, like a volume of miscellany, without an index—or rather like a dictionary, to be looked into on occasions, but without any connexion. The following sketches I have extracted from his Diary,—a very wilderness of unintelligible chirography. I think there is some merit in them. There is, at least, originality.   J.G.W.

94

AT HOME – AN APRIL DAY

Rain–rain!–no, not precisely rain,–but worse, infinitely worse–an April day of mist and shadow,–such as Ossian's ghosts might revel in,–mud and water below, cloud-rack and moisture above!–Faugh!–Coleridge says that the mind gives nature its gloom and its beauty–its light and sombre coloring. No such thing. Nature colors the mind. I feel at this moment her shadows closing around me. I am out of humor with her. It seems to me as if she has assumed her most dreary and uncomfortable aspect for my own especial annoyance. I can have some patience with a thunder-storm. There is something of grandeur about it,–the slow, uprolling clouds–the lightning flashing out of their thick blackness, like the eye-glance of an angry spirit--the solemn roll of the far-off thunder–or the simultaneous flash and uproar, as some hill-crag or tree-top trembles with its fiery chastisement. A sweeping Northeaster is a disagreeable visitant; but within doors you can easily reconcile yourself to it; and there is somewhat of amusement in the gusty clashing of the rain–the flooding of the streets–the swaying of the tree-tops–the rending of umbrellas, and the forlorn appearance of the cloak-wrapped pedestrians. But a dull, heavy, clinging mist–a day of cloud and shadow, when Nature seems puzzled whether to rain or shine upon us–is the peculiar season when the azure demons of my temperament hold high carnival. If I ever commit suicide, commend me to such a day.

Is *that* my face–hirsute, sallow, ghastly!–peering out upon me, like ugliness personified, from that long, old-fashioned mirror?–I will have that perpetual *memento mori* turned to the wall. I dislike *reflections* of any kind. I enter my solemn protest against looking-glasses in modern days, as Pliny and Seneca did of old. One of the Roman Emperors–Domitian, I believe, lined his galleries and walks with polished selenite, that he might see all that was going on around him. The man was a fool. For my own part, I could abide the daily risque of assassination, with far more composure, than the constant vision of my unlucky figure. In the latter case, I should imagine myself haunted by an ogre.

I hate your professed Physiognomist–the man who reads at a glance the character of his neighbor–decyphering with ease the mystic meaning of the human features—those hieroglyphics of the Almighty. I abhor the idea of a man's carrying his autobiography in his visage--the melancholy history of a love adventure in the droop of an eye-lid, or the prominence of a cheek-bone,—or a tale of disappointment in the wrinkles of his forehead. I condemn *in toto* the systems of **Lavater, Gall,** and **S**purzheim. 'Tis an unmanly method of coming at one's private history. The beautiful and lordly—those who carry an eternal letter of recommendation in their countenances—may, perhaps, demur to my opinions. Let them. Phrenology may have been a blessing to them; it has been the devil and all to me.

As Balak said of old unto Balaam,—so say I unto all, who, like myself have been martyrs to the sciences of bumps, organs, and facial angles—Physiogonomy and Phrenology—"Come, help me to curse them." Nay, smile not at my vehemence, fair reader; thou least of all canst appreciate my feelings. As thou bendest over my page, with thine eye shedding a finer light across it than ever brightened the illuminated scroll of a monkish legend--with thy dark tresses ever and anon lightly sweeping its margin, and half shadowing the delicate fingers which enclose it—the veriest mocker at humanity would bless thee, and the austere St. Francis, at the first glimpse of thee, would have forsaken his bride of snow. But I, marked and set apart from my fellows, the personification of ugliness, in whose countenance every modern Lavater discovers all that is vile and disagreeable and odious; shunned by the lovelier and gentler sex, and suspected and laughed at by my own; in the name of all that is sensitive, why should I not murmur at the practice of an art which has undone me, at the illustration of a science which has shut the door of human sympathy upon me! Is it a light thing that I have suffered a daily martyrdom through life; that my very parents loved me not, although my young heart was bursting with love for them; that my brothers mocked me, and my sisters feared me; that, in my riper years, the one fair being to whom I poured out the riches of a hoarded affection, the whole of that love which had been turned back and repelled by all others—that she, who *did* love me, who saw through its miserable veil of humanity, the warm and generous and lofty spirit within me—even *she* should have been torn from me by those who knew me not, save by that most unfortunate criterion of merit, my outward appearance? Is it nothing that I am now a lonely and disappointed man, stricken into the "sere and yellow leaf," before my time, with the frost of misery if not of years predominating over the dark locks of my boyhood? Is it nothing that I am not a solitary wanderer in the thoroughfare of being; my sympathies fettered down in my own bosom, my affections unshared, unreciprocated, and wandering like the winged messenger of the Patriarch of the deluge over the broad waste of an unsocial humanity; and, finding no rest, no place of refuge, no beautiful island in the eternal solitude, no green-branched forest looking above the desolation, where the weary wing may be folded, and the fainting heart have rest?

Basta!—I have been penning nonsense, sheer inexcusable nonsense; and yet, it has brought moisture to my eye, and a tremor to my heart. I'faith! I should like to see a tear of mine. It is a very long, time since I saw one. *Manhood in its desolation has no tears.* "Woman-kind," says King James, the old Scotch pedant, "especially bee able to shede teares at everie light occasion, when they will—yea, although it were dissemblingly, like the crocodiles." And Reginald Scott affirmeth, "there bee two kindes of teares in woman's eie; one of true greefe, the other of deceipt." Well, it is a happy faculty, this tear-shedding, after all. It is a woman's last and most powerful appeal. There are few hearts capable of resisting it. It excites pity, and pity, by gradations almost insensible, melts into love. I have often admired the truth of a remark in Godwin's Cloudesly. "Beauty in tears is the adversary which has thrown down its weapons, and no longer defies us. It is the weak and tender flower, illustrious in its lowliness, which asks for a friendly hand to raise its drooping head."

Rain, rain—drip, drip! fog wrapping the hills like a winding sheet. And here am I, sitting by my dim and whitening coal-fire, a wretched misanthrope—a combination of the ferocity of Timon and the spleen of Rochefoucauld. Solitary, companionless:—

"Alone, alone! All, all alone!"

No beautiful creature of smiles and gentle tones to cheer my failing spirits, and melt away the sternness of care with the warm kiss of her affection. But wherefore these murmurs? Matrimony,

97

after all, is but a doubtful experiment. What saith my Lord Bacon? "He that hath wife and children hath given hostages to fortune; for they are impediments to great enterprizes, either of virtue or mischief. Certainly the best works, and of greatest merit to the public, have proceeded from unmarried and childless men." And Count Swedenborg, for whom I have a great veneration, thinks that woman is to man like the lost rib to Adam, not essential to his happiness, but necessary to complete his fortune." In truth, I can readily conceive of a worse situation than my own. I might have married,—I shudder to think of it,—a scold, a termagant, a Xantippe, (and now I remember that she did have a wonderful faculty of sharpening her fine voice.) Our old law Latin most ungallantly confines the common scold, *communis vixatix*, to the feminine gender; and the Furies were all represented as females. For one, I value a fine and pleasant voice as the most perfect charm of women. I would have it soft, low and faintly musical, like the straying of the south wind over harp-strings—an articulate breathing, mellowed and rich with the earnestness of soul, soothing and gentle as the whisper of an angel. The ancients represented Venus by the side of Mercury, to signify that the chief pleasures of matrimony were in conversation. I have ever admired these lines of old Ausonius:

"Van quid affectas faciem mihi pingere pictor?
Si mihi similem pingere, pinge sonum."

And it is thus I would have my "lodge love" delineated, not upon perishing canvass, but on the retina of the soul;

"The voiceless spirit of a lovely sound."

But, the common scold—the razor-like voice of petulance and anger, piercing through one like a Toledo scimetar, the curtain lecture, the domestic brawl, the harsh tones of taunting and menace, the sawmill modulation of vulgarity—Heaven defend me from them!

With the honest weaver of Auchinoloch, "I hae muckle reason to be thankful that I am, as I am." Rubius Celer, indeed, commanded the fact to be engraven on his tomb-stone, that he had lived with his wife Caja Ennia forty-three years and eight months, without any domestic quarrel. But his is a solitary case. I am half inclined to believe that the immaculate Caja Ennia was dumb.

I know of nothing which has given me more consolation in my bachelorship, than the song of Vidal, in one of the Scott's Romances:

> "Woman's faith, and woman's trust—
> Write the characters in dust,—
> Print them on the running stream,
> Stamp them on the cold moon-beam,
> And each evanescent letter
> Shall be fairer, firmer, better,
> And more durable, I ween,
> Than the thing those letters mean."

It is unquestionably a propensity of the human heart, to seek to depreciate that, which it has in vain sought after, and it may be owing to this, that I take such malicious satisfaction in contemplating the character of our mother Eve. She loved Adam awhile in Paradise, it is true; but the very "first devil she saw, she changed her love."

POETRY — REMINISCENCE — LORD BYRON

"World! stop thy mouth—I am resolved to rhyme!" So sung Peter Pindar—but so sing not I. Time has dealt hardly with my boyhood's muse. Poetry has been to me a beautiful delusion. It was something woven of my young fancies, and reality has destroyed it. I can, indeed, make rhymes now, as mechanically as a mason piles one brick above another; but the glow of feeling, the hope, the ardor, the excitement have passed away forever. I have long thought, or rather the world hath *made* me think, that poetry is too trifling, too insignificant a pursuit for the matured intellect of sober manhood. I have half acquiesced in the opinion of Plato, who banished poets from his ideal republic. I could have

99

assisted Gregory the Great in his celebrated *Auto da fe* of the old Latin authors. Adam Ferguson, in his Essays on Civil Society, argues conclusively, that man, in his savage and heathen state, is by nature a poet; and it was probably the knowledge of this fact, which induced the early Christians of Greece, according to Petrus Bellonius, a voracious Basil Hall of antiquity, to esteem it not lawful for a Christian to study poetry.

I have been looking over a confused map of my old manuscripts—like Ovid's Chaos,

"A huge and undigested heap."

Each particular scrap has something pleasant or mournful associated with its history. There is one written by a friend who has long since "shuffled off this mortal coil." Poor fellow! "the clods of the valley are sweet to him," for he was, in truth, one of those "who rejoice exceedingly, and are glad when they can find the grave." I think I can see him now, pale, spiritually pale, with his large blue eyes, and his most melancholy smile. He died early; but I could not mourn for him, for his spirit longed for rest, "as the servant earnestly desireth the shadow." To him might have been applied the mournful language of the son of Sirach: "Oh Death, acceptable is thy sentence unto the needy, unto him whose strength faileth, who is vexed with all things, and to him who despaireth, and hath lost all patience." The following stanzas were written shortly after an afflicting bereavement. I regard them not for their intrinsic merit, but as the production of one whom I have loved.

Fare thee well! if this be only
    As a lightly-spoken word,
Wherefore should this heart be lonely
    As a mate-forsaken bird?
If its meaning be not deeper
    Than its simple sound would seem,
Wherefore should it haunt the sleeper,
    Like a murmur in his dream?

Lowly was the cold word spoken,
　　With a pale and trembling lip,
When the chance of earth had broken
　　On our early fellowship.
Pale the stars were bending o'er us—
　　Emblems of thy rare charms,
And the streamlet ran before us
　　With the moonlight in its arms!

With the brilliant tear-drop starting
　　From thy fringing eye-lid forth,
Like a summoned angel parting
　　With a weary son of earth,—
Still in slumber I behold thee,
　　Even as we parted there,—
But the arms that would enfold thee
　　Clasp the cold and vacant air!

Quiet is thy place of sleeping,
　　In a brighter clime than ours,
Where the island-palm is keeping
　　Watch above thy funeral flowers:
And the tall Magnolia lingers
　　Near thee, with its snowy blossom,
That the breeze, like love's own fingers,
　　Scatters o'er thy sleeping bosom.

Fare thee well!—my heart is near thee,
　　And its love is still as deep,
While the soul can see and hear thee,
　　In the dreamy hour of sleep:
Dear one!—be thy blessing o'er me,
　　And thy sinless spirit given,
As an angel-guide before me,
　　Leading upward unto Heaven!

Well might my poor friend lament thus passionately the loss of
the fairest and best of earth's daughters! Years have passed
since I saw her for the last time, on the eve of her departure for

Cuba--her native island. Sickness had begun its work on her delicate frame; but the spiritual loveliness of her countenance I shall never forget. Her eye would have answered to the inimitable description of Sterne: —"It was an eye full of gentle salutations and soft responses—speaking not like the trumpet-stop of an ill-made organ, in which many an eye I talk to, holds coarse converse—but whispering soft, like the last, low accents of an expiring saint." I have the copy of some lines written on the eve of her departure, by her poetical lover. I know not how they may seem to others—to me they are commended by the earnestness of affection which they manifest.

> Clara! this hand is thrilling yet,
>   With the last pressure of thine own.
> Oh! could my aching heart forget
>   The sadness of thy parting tone,—
> Could but the pale lip pass away—
>   Thy thin cheek lose its hectic stain,
> And, bright and beautiful and gay,
>   Thy treasured image smile again
> Upon me, as it once hath smiled,—
>   Could once again thine aspect find
> The healthful beauty of a child,
>   Blest with the holier charm of mind,—
> I would not ask a dream of bliss
> More holy, pure, and deep, than this!
>
> Yet go—I would not keep thee here,
>   When sickness dims thine eye's pure heaven,—
> Go—seek thy natal atmosphere,
>   Where steals the breath of morn and even,
> Like soft and healing balm, along
>   The sunny waves and orange bowers,
> Rich with the silver voice of song,
>   And fragrant with the kiss of flowers!
> Go—and beneath that warm bright sky,
>   May healing spirits hover o'er thee,
> Until, beneath thy kindling eye,
>   The world again is bright before thee;

And cheek and lip again possess
Their more than mortal loveliness!

Go—and I need not ask of thee
    A thought—a prayer—a silent blessing,
Nor that our plighted love may be
    The holiest gift of thy possessing
I know too well thy gentle heart
    To wrong thee by one selfish fear,—
And, freely as I weep to part,
    No doubt hath summoned up a tear.
God's blessing on thee! —If the prayer
    Of a fond heart availeth much,
He, whose pervading love can spare
    The loveliest flower from ruin's touch,
Will spare thee in thy native bower,
As being's best and loveliest flower!

I have been reading Byron to day—following him through the classic ground of Europe, and blending myself in sympathy with his heroes,—bending with Conrad over the dim waste of waters,—leaning with Laura gloomily against the pillars of the banquet-room—dark and alone, amidst light and love and music,—scowling with the Giaour in the dim aisle of the convent,—

"With gloom beheld—with gloom beholding
The rites which sanctify the pile."

I have gazed with Alp, while the cloud of his destiny swept darkly between him and heaven,—or looked with Manfred from "the difficult air of the iced mountain-top"—down where the mist boiled upward from the valleys—

——"white and sulphurous,
Like foam from the roused ocean of deep hell,
Heaped with the damned like pebbles."

Byron is no more, nobly he perished in the classic land of his

103

adoption, where

> ———"The mountains look on Marathon
> And Marathon looks on the sea."

He sleeps well, "after life's fitful fever;" and God forbid that any one should wantonly attack his memory. I admire—I almost worship the sublimity of his genius. I would not, if it were in the power of man to do so, detract one tittle from the full measure of his great fame. But I have feared—and still fear—the consequences—the natural and unavoidable consequences of his writings. I fear that, in our enthusiastic admiration of genius, our idolatry of poetry, the allurements to vice and loathsome depravity, the awful impiety, and the staggering unbelief contained in those writings, are lightly passed over, and acquiesced in, as the allowable observations of a master intellect, which had lifted itself above the ordinary world, which had broken down the barriers of ordinary mind, and which revelled in a creation of his own; a world, over which the sunshine of imagination lightened, at times, with an almost ineffable glory, to be succeeded by the thick blackness of doubt and terror and misanthropy, relieved only by the lightening flashes of terrible and unholy passion.

The blessing of that mighty intellect—the prodigal gift of Heaven—became, in his possession, a burthen and a curse. He was wretched in his gloomy unbelief, and he strove, with that selfish purpose which too often actuates the miserable, to drag his fellow-beings from their only abiding hope—to break down in the human bosom the beautiful altar of its faith, and to fix in other bosoms the doubt and despair which darkened his own,--to lead his readers—the vast multitude of the beautiful, the pure and the gifted, who knelt to his genius as to the manifestations of a new divinity—into that ever darkened path which is trodden only by the lost to hope—the forsaken of Heaven—and which leads from the perfect light of holiness down to the shadows of eternal death.

If ever man possessed the power of controlling at will the passions of his readers, that man was Lord Byron. He knew and felt the mightiness of this power—and he loved its exercise—to kindle in a thousand bosoms the strange fire which desolated his own. He loved to shake down with a giant's strength the strongest pillars of human confidence—to unfix the young and susceptible spirit from its allegiance to virtue and to the dearest ties of nature. No man ever drew finer and more enchanting pictures of the social virtues—and love and friendship never seem more beautiful than when made the subject of his vivid and graphic delineation. But a cold sneer of scepticism, and an unfeeling turn of expression, or a vulgar and disgusting companion associated with images of purity and loveliness, breaks in upon the delicious reverie of the reader, like a foul satyr in the companionship of angels; and the holiness of beauty departs—the sweet spell is broken forever, and the sacred image of virtue is associated with disgust and abhorrence. It seems as if the mighty magician delighted in adorning with the sun-like hues of his imagination the Paradise of Virtue, in order to discover more fully the fell power which he possessed, of darkening and defacing the fair vision, of sending the curse of his own perverted feelings to brood over it, like the wing of a destroying angel.

What, for instance, can be more beautiful—more deeply imbued with the genuine spirit of pure and holy love, than the epistle of Julia to her lover, in Don Juan! Yet to whom are these sentiments attributed? To a vile and polluted paramour—an adulteress; to a bosom glowing not with the ethereal principle of love, but with the fires of a consuming and guilty passion. They should have emanated from a heart as pure and unsullied as the descending snow-flakes, before one stain of earth had dimmed its original purity.

Genius—the pride of genius—what is there in it, after all, to take the precedence of virtue? Why should we worship the hideousness of vice, although the glowing drapery of angel be gathered about it? In the awful estimate of eternity, what is the fame of a Shakespeare to the beautiful humility of a heart sanctified by the approval of the Searcher of all bosoms? The lowliest taster of the pure and living waters of religion is "a better and wiser man," than the deepest quaffer at the fount of Helicon; and the humble follower of that sublime philosophy of heaven, which the pride of the human heart accounteth foolishness, is greater and worthier than the skilled in human science, whose learning and glory only enable them—"*Sapienter ad infernum descendere.*"

AMERICAN ROMANCE

It has often been said that the New World is deficient in poetry
and romance; that its bards must of necessity linger over the
the classic ruins of other lands; and draw their sketches of character from foreign sources, and paint Nature under the soft beauty
of an Eastern sky. On the contrary, New England is full of
Romance. The great forest which our fathers penetrated—the red
men—their struggle and their disappearance—the Powwow and the
War-dance—the savage inroad and the English sally—the tale of
superstition, and the scenes of Witchcraft; all these are rich
materials of poetry. We have indeed no classic vale of Tempe—
no haunted Parnassus—no temple, gray with years, and hallowed
by the gorgeous pageantry of idol worship—no towers and castles
over whose moonlight ruins gathers the green pall of the ivy.
But we have mountains pillaring a sky as blue as that which
bends over classic Olympus: streams as bright and beautiful as
those of Greece or Italy—and forests richer and nobler than those
which of old were haunted by Sylph and Dryad.

J. G. Whittier

The Bouquet, Hartford, October 6, 1832

AMERICAN WRITERS

As an American, I am proud of the many gifted spirits who
have laid their offerings upon the altar of our national literature.
I believe them capable of greater and more successful efforts.
I would encourage them onward. There is a growing disposition
at home and abroad to reward literary exertion. And even if such
were not the fact, is there nothing in the mild process of intellectual refinement, which is of itself worth more than the great
world can bestow? 'Poetry,' says Coleridge, 'has been to me its

own exceeding great reward.' This consciousness of rightly improving the endowments of heaven—of possessing a pure, internal
fountain of innocent happiness, to which the spirit may turn for
its refreshing, from the fever of the world—this contented self
reliance,

> 'Which nothing earthly gives, or can destroy,
> The soul's calm sunshine and the heartfelt joy'

is far more to be desired than the deceitful murmurs of applause
falling upon the craving ear of an unsatisfied spirit. Goethe
learned this truth, long before the public eye was fixed upon
him. He could be happy and satisfied in the enjoyment of his own
intellectual paradise, even before the world had realized or acknowledged its exceeding beauty. In such a state, the mind becomes worthy of its origin. It realizes in Time, something of the
expansion in Eternity.

J. G. Whittier

The Bouquet, Hartford, October 6, 1832

NEW ENGLAND SUPERSTITIONS

> — 'Tis a history
> Handed from ages down; a nurse's tale —
> Which children, open-eyed and mouthed, devour;
> We learn it and believe.   Thalaha.

An elegant writer in a late number of the New England magazine, has given us an interesting and philosophical essay upon
popular superstitions; and made particular allusion to those which
may be considered peculiar to, or prevalent in, New England. I
cannot but wish, that some of our writers, (and I know of no one
better qualified to perform the tasks than the gentleman I have
alluded to,) could be induced to embody and illustrate such passages of superstition, as may be considered in any way peculiar
to the New World. Our fathers had a theory of their own in rela-

tion to the invisible world—in which they had united, by a most natural process, the wild and extravagant mysteries of their savage neighbors, with the old and common superstitions of their native land; and that stern, gloomy, indefinite awe of an agency of evil, which their peculiar interpretations of the sacred volume had inspired; a theory, which mingled with and had a practical effect upon their habits and dispositions,—which threw a veil of mystery over the plainest passages of the great laws of the universe,—which gave a constraint and an awe to their intercourse with one another,—agitating the whole community with signs and wonders, and dark marvels,—poisoning the fountains of education, —and constituting a part of their religion.

The principal relics of these ancient superstitions, which still linger with us, may be classed under the following heads:

I *Haunted Houses.* By which is not always understood the actual appearance of a spirit from the dead; but, not unfrequently, a super-natural disturbance—noises in the deep midnight—the revelling of evil demons, etc.

I have heard but little of haunted houses in this vicinity for some time past. Our Yankee thrift, in truth, does not often allow us to keep houses for the accomodation of such ghostly tenants as never pay for their lodgings. One of my neighbors formerly complained a good deal of the disturbing revels which ghosts or witches nightly got up under his roof. All night long he could hear a dance moving lightly to the tune of some infernal melody:

> Where hornpipes, jigs, strathspeys and reels
> Put life and mettle in the heels.

of the unseen revelers. Latterly, however, I learn that his tormentors have given him a respite.

II *Ghosts.* The appearance of a departed friend or enemy; a visible similitude of the dead, revealed to the living only upon some extraordinary contingency; to publish like that of "Buried Denmark," some "foul and most unnatural murder" or injury; to settle without fee disputes between the heirs of the dead man's property, and for various other "wicked or charitable purposes."

III *Witches.* Including male and female under the same general term. This class of worthies is getting very much out of repute. In the county of Essex, which was formerly their headquarters, there is not a single survivor, worthy of the name; although we have many most devout believers in their potency. Kingston, New Hampshire, has been somewhat celebrated for a family of witches. Two elderly sisters used, a few years since, to be seen winding their way to market, with a few small baskets of their own manufacture, mounted on horses as lean as their skeleton riders, the objects of great terror to all the urchins of the street. They were evil, malicious, malignant, and their appearance involuntarily reminded one of Otway's famous descriptive in his "Orphan":–

"I spied a withered hag with age grown double,
Picking dry sticks, and mumbling to herself;
Her eyes with scalding rheum were galled and red,
Cold palsy shook her head, her hands seemed withered,
And on her crooked shoulders, had she wrapped
The tattered remnants of an old striped hanging,
Which served to keep her carcass from the cold."

They are now, I believe, both dead. A person who attended the funeral of one of them, told me, with great gravity, that the coffin of her, who, when living, was seemingly as unsubstantial as the ghosts of Ossian, through which the stars were visible, was at first so heavy that eight stout men could not raise it; but, that after waiting a while for the *spell* to be removed, it could be easily taken up by a single man.

IV *Fortune-telling.* This is still considerably practiced; not so much, however, by the professed disciples of astrology and palmistry, as by the younger classes of our inland community. It is usually called *trying projects;* very much like those described by Burns, in his inimitable Halloween.

V *Warnings of Death or Disaster.* This species of superstition is completely inwrought. It has most successfully resisted the operations of science and philosophy.

A very honest and intelligent neighbor of mine, once told me that at the precise moment when his brother was drowned in the Merrimac, many miles distant, he felt a sudden and painful sensation,–a death-like chill upon his heart, such as he had never before experienced. I have heard many similar relations. Those

109

who have read Walton's life of Donne, will recollect the theory of that quaint and excellent old author on this subject; that there is a sympathy of soul,—an electric chain of mental affinity —upon which the emotions of one spirit thrill and tremble even to another.

VI *Spectres*. I use this term in the sense in which it was made to apply, during the memorable era of 1692, to the appearance or phantom of a living person, who, at the time of its visitation, is known to be absent. Such appearances are supposed to denote the speedy death of the person whom they represent.

A widow lady, residing in an adjoining town, is clearly convinced that she saw the spectre of her daughter a little time before her death, yet when she was in perfect health. It crossed the room within a few feet of the mother, and in broad day-light. She spoke; but no answer was returned; the countenance of the apparition was fixed and sorrowful. The daughter was at the time absent on a visit to a friend.

VII *Supposed Preternatural Appearances*. Unconnected with any circumstances peculiar to those who witness them; lights dancing in lonely places and graveyards, meteors, etc., etc. These are usually denominated *sights*.

I have listened, hour after hour, of a winter's evening, to minute descriptions of these appearances. A much-lamented friend of mine,—a sober and intelligent farmer,—once informed me, that, while engaged in sledding rails for his spring fence, many years since, his team suddenly stood still, apparently unable to proceed. It was a night of cold, clear moonshine; the path was smooth and slippery as glass; and the pause made about midway in the descent of a hill. He examined the runners on all sides, but no obstruction was apparent. He lifted up the runners in front, and urged forward his oxen at the same time; the cattle exerted their whole strength—the very bows of their yoke cracked with the effort; but the sled remained immovable, as if bedded in a solid rock. After repeated trials had been made, and the farmer was on the point of leaving his sled for the night, a sharp report like that of a pistol was heard—a strong blaze of fire enveloped the whole team; and the sled instantly glided down the declivity with a speed which greatly embarrassed the oxen, which but a moment before had in vain endeavored to move it.

The farmer had never probably read Coleridge's poetical description of a somewhat similar detention of the ship of the "Ancient Mariner," which, held by the demon, in the teeth of the wind, kept swaying and struggling

> "Backwards and forwards, half her length,
> With a short, uneasy motion;"

and which, when released at last,

> "Like a pawing horse set free,
> Sprang forth with sudden bound;"

yet the *experimentum crucis*, whereby he attempted to ascertain the cause of such an extraordinary circumstance, led him to ascribe it to witchcraft, or some other supernatural agency. There were facts to be explained, which, in his opinion, could only refer themselves to such a cause.

A pond in my vicinity has been somewhat celebrated for its "sights and marvels." A middle-aged lady of good intelligence, residing near it, states, that one summer evening, between daylight and dark, while standing by the side of the highway, leading along the margin of the pond, she was startled by the appearance of a horse, attached to an old-fashioned cart, and driven by an elderly man, plunging at full speed down the hill which rises abruptly from the water, and over a rough pasture where it would seem impossible for a vehicle to be conveyed. It passed swiftly and noiselessly over the high wall bounding the pasture without displacing a stone, and crossed the street within a few yards of the astonished looker-on. Behind the cart, and bound to it by a strong rope, fastened to her wrists, a woman of gigantic stature was dragged furiously onward, writhing like Lacoon in the clasp of the serpent. Her feet, head, and arms were naked; and grey locks of wild hair streamed back from temples corrugated and darkened. The horrible cavalcade swept by, and disappeared in the thick swamp which touches the western extremity of the pond.

I could mention half a dozen other places within a few miles of my residence, equally celebrated for the "unco" sights and sounds which have been seen or heard near them. The Devil's

Den, in Chester, N. H. is among the most prominent in this respect. How his satanic majesty came in possession of it, I have never been able to ascertain; but that it is a favorite resort of his, is incontestibly proved by the fact, that he always keeps a smooth foot-track to its entrance, whether in summer or winter. The following rhymes, if they answer no other purpose, will serve to show that the place and its legend are enjoying as comfortable a chance of immortality as Yankee poetry can give them. (The poem is Whittier's own early Gothic piece *The Demon's Cave.)*

"The moon is bright on the rocky hill,
But its dwarfish pines rise gloomily still,—
Fixed, motionless forms in the silent air,
The moonlight is on them, but darkness is there.
The drowsy flap of the owlet's wing,
And the stream's low gush from its hidden spring,
And the passing breeze, in its flight betrayed
By the timid shiver of leaf and blade,
Half like a sigh and half a moan,
The ear of the listener catches alone.

A dim cave yawns in the rude hill-side
Like the jaws of a monster opened wide,
Where a few wild bushes of thorn and fern
Their leaves from the breath of the night-air turn;
And half with the twining foliage cover
The mouth of that shadowy cavern over:—
Above it, the rock hangs gloomy and high,
Like a rent in the blue of the beautiful sky,
Which seems, as it opens on either hand,
Like some bright sea leaving a desolate land.

Below it, a stream on its bed of stone
From a rift in the rock comes hurrying down,
Telling forever the same wild tale
Of its loftier home to the lowly vale:
And over its waters an oak is bending,
Its boughs like a skeleton's arms extending,—
A naked tree, by the lightning shorn,

112

With its trunk all bare and its branches torn;
And the rocks beneath it, blackened and rent,
Tell where the bolt of the thunder went.

'Tis said that this cave is an evil place
The chosen haunt of the fallen race—
That the midnight traveller oft hath seen
A red flame tremble its jaws between,
And lighten and quiver the boughs among,
Like the fiery play of a serpent's tongue;
That sounds of fear from its chamber's swell—
The ghostly gibber,—the fiendish yell;
That bodiless hands at its entrance wave,—
And hence they have named it the Demon's Cave!

The fears of man to this place have lent
A terror which Nature never meant;—
For who hath wandered, with curious eye
This dim and shadowy cavern by,
And known, in the sun or star-light, aught
Which might not beseem so lovely a spot,—
The stealthy fox, and the shy raccoon—
The night-bird's wing in the shining moon—
The frog's low croak; and, upon the hill,
The steady chant of the whipporwill?

Yet is there something to fancy dear
In this silent cave and its lingering fear,—
Something which tells of another age,
Of the wizard's wand, and the Sybil's page,
Of the fairy ring and the haunted glen,
And the restless phantoms of murdered men:
The grandame's tale, and the nurse's song—
The dreams of childhood remembered long;
And I love even now to list the tale
Of the Demon's Cave, and its haunted vale."*

*Cp. Frances M. Pray. "A Study of Whittier's Apprenticeship as
A Poet," Bristol, N. H., 1930, pp. 68-9.

113

One of the most striking instances of the effects of a disordered imagination recently occurred in this vicinity. The following are the facts:

In September, 1831, a worthy and highly esteemed inhabitant of this town died suddenly on the bridge over the Merrimac, by the bursting of a blood-vessel. It was just at day-break, when he was engaged with another person in raising the draw of the bridge for the passage of a sloop. The suddenness of the event; the excellent character of the deceased; and, above all, a vague rumor, that some extraordinary disclosure was to be made, drew together a large concourse at the funeral. After the solemn services were concluded, Thomas, the brother of the dead man,—himself a most exemplary Christian,—rose up, and desired to relate some particulars regarding the death of his brother. He then stated,—and his manner calm, solemn, impressive,—that, more than a month previous to his death, his brother had told him, that his feelings had been painfully disturbed by seeing, at different times, on the bridge, a quantity of human blood;—that, sometimes while he was gazing upon it, it suddenly disappeared, as if removed by an invisible hand; that it lay thick and dark amidst the straw and litter; that, many times, in the dusk of the evening, he had seen a vessel coming down the river, which vanished just as it reached the draw; and that, at the same time, he had heard a voice calling in a faint and lamentable tone— *I am dying* and that the voice sounded like his own; that then he knew that the vision was for him, and that his hour of departure was at hand. Thomas, moreover, stated that, a few days before the melancholy event took place, his brother, after assuring him that he would be called upon to testify to the accounts which he had given of the vision on the bridge, told him that he had actually seen the same vessel go up the river, whose spectral image he had seen in his vision, and that, when it returned, the fatal fulfilment would take place; that, night after night, he had heard what seemed to him the sound of the horn from that vessel, calling for the raising of the draw, and that it was to him very solemn and awful. "You all know," continued the narrator, "how my brother died,—that he died fulfilling the vision,—that his blood lies even now upon the bridge, as *he* saw it before his death; and that his last words were heard by the captain of the vessel—'*I am dying!*' "

There was something in the circumstances of this narration,—the church crowded with faces bent earnestly on the speaker,—the evident sincerity, and deep solemnity of the narrator,—and the fearful character of his communication,—while the yet unburied corpse of his brother lay before him,—which was calculated to revive every latent feeling of superstition; and to overpower, at least for the moment, the convictions of reason and the arguments of philosophy.

It is altogether foreign to my purpose to enter into any deliberate analysis of the nature of these superstitions. I have briefly alluded to a few instances, of my own neighborhood and times, for the purpose of showing that, even in our enlightened age and community, the delusions of the past still linger around us; and that there is no lack of materials for an amusing and not uninstructing work of the character I have already mentioned in the beginning of this article.

J. G. W.

Haverhill, 1st of 6th mo., 1833

New England Magazine, July, 1833.

ELIZABETH B. BARRETT

The name of this eminently gifted lady is as yet unfamiliar to American ears. With a range and variety of genius and acquirements far beyond those of the popular Frederika Bremer, or the fascinating Mary Howitt, she has been hitherto known only as the author of a few exquisite lyrics and some admirable prose articles on the "Greek Christian Poets." She is an invalid—confined entirely to her apartment; and in such an extremely delicate state of health as to be rarely seen by any except her own family. She has already endured six or seven years of such imprisonment, with resignation, serenity, and warm sympathies toward the world from which she has been so long excluded. She is a remarkable student. She has read Plato in the original, the Hebrew and Chaldean tongues are familiar to her; and, to use the words of the author of the "New Spirit of the Age," there is probably not a single good romance of the most romantic kind, in whose marvelous and impossible scenes she has not delighted.

A couple of volumes from her pen, entitled "A Drama of Life, and Other Poems," has just been put to the press in England, the proof sheets of which have been sent to a New York publishers. The last number of the Democratic Review contains the opening part of the "Drama of Life," a poem on the Fall of Our First Parents—daringly treading the path of Milton, not as a servile imitator, but with much of the same power of imagination, which enabled the blind bard of Paradise to overlook the walls of angel-guarded Eden, to pass the pearl-gates of the City of God, and tread with the Archangel ruined the hot marl of the Place of Pain, arched over by eternal fire. The Review speaks of this poem as the finest which has appeared since Byron's "Manfred."

The Drama opens with a dialogue between Gabriel and Lucifer immediately after the curse had been pronounced upon the sinners, and the guilty pair were fleeing from the glare of the fiery sword at the entrance of their lost Paradise. This is followed by the song of the Spirits of Eden, sending their mournful and upbraiding notes of farewell after the unhappy fugitives. Our limited space will not allow us to make copious extracts, but we cannot forbear copying the following exquisite lament:

Chorus of Eden Spirits.
(Chanting from Paradise, while Adam and Eve fly across the sword-glare.)

Harken, oh harken! let your souls behind you,
Lean gentle moved!

(About nine inches of quotation from the poem concludes the review.)

The Middlesex Standard, Lowell, Mass., July 25, 1844.

IT IS NEVER TOO LATE

(Frederika Bremer)

"AH! that I could be heard by all the oppressed, dejected souls! I would cry to them —"Lift up your head; and confide still in the future, and believe that it is never too late!" — See! I too was bowed down by long suffering, and old age had moreover overtaken me, and I believed that all my strength had vanished:– that my life and my sufferings were in vain— and behold! my head had again been lifted up, my heart appeased, my soul strengthened; and now, in my fiftieth year, I advance into a new future, attended by all that life has of beautiful and worthy of love.

"The change in my soul has enabled me better to comprehend life and suffering, and I am now firmly convinced that there is no fruitless suffering, and that no virtuous endeavor is in vain. Winter days and nights may bury beneath their pall of snow the sown corn; but when the spring arrives, it will be found equally true, that "there grows much bread in the winter night."

(Printer's hand) There are truth, and power, and beauty in the above extract from the writings of the gifted Frederika Bremer. It is worthy the attention of every one who feels the load of life growing heavy, and who is ready to cry out "my burden is greater than I can bear." The great secret of rising above sorrow, of conquering misfortune, of reconciling disappointments, is to be found in a resolution to do good to others— to make others happy. Once firmly entered upon, this resolution will save us. In the pure and healthful excitement of some great and good object of benevolence and duty, we forget ourselves, and our sufferings; the weary woe which has been settling around our hearts melts away like mist in the sunshine; the troubled and haunting thoughts which have maddened us give place to "the peace which passeth understanding."

Frederika Bremer has experienced all this - and hence her ability to "minister to minds diseased." —She has made herself happy while contributing to the intellectual enjoyment of others— and her writings, especially her admirable "Strife and Peace" are

117

characterized by democratic sentiment, and a clear appreciation of the equal claims of humanity. She is a decided ABOLITIONIST; and, like her gifted English sister Harriet Martineau, evinces a deep interest in the progress of anti-slavery sentiment in America.

Ed. Standard.

Middlesex Standard, Lowell, Mass., August 1, 1844.

ALEXANDER PUSHKIN

On the 29th of the 1st month, 1837, in one of the stately mansions of the Northern Capital, on the banks of the Neva, a great man lay dying. The rooms which led to the chamber of suffering were thronged with the wealthy, the titled, the gifted, of St. Petersburg, anxiously inquiring after the condition of the sufferer. A great light was going out. Alexander Pushkin—the poet and historian, the favorite alike of Emperor and people—stricken in a fatal duel two days before, lay waiting for his summons to the world of spirits. And when, at last, the weeping Jukovskii *(sic)*, himself only second to Pushkin as a poet, announced to the anxious crowds in attendance, that his friend was no more, prince and peasant bowed their heads in sorrow. The cold heart of the North was touched with the pang of a great bereavement. The poet of Russia, the only man of the age who could wear with honor the mantles of Derzhavin and Karamsin, had passed beneath that shadow, "the light whereof is darkness."

Now, who was Alexander Pushkin? Can it be possible that this man, so wonderfully gifted, so honoured, so lamented, was a colored man—a negro? Such, it seems, is the fact, incredible as it may appear to the American reader. His maternal grandfather was a negro, named Annibal, who was patronized by the Czar, and became an officer in the marine service. Of his African origin Pushkin bore, in his personal appearance and mental characteristics, the most unequivocal marks. An article in Blackwood, for the 6th month, 1845, describes him as follows:

"The closely curled every hair, the mobile and irre-

118

gular features, the darkness of his complexion, all betrayed his African descent, and served as an appropriate outside to his character."

At an early age, Pushkin became a pupil in the Imperial Lyceum, then recently established and richly endowed by Alexander. While here, the young man, after reciting one of his pieces, on a public occasion, was pronounced a *poet* by the aged Derzhavin, the author of the sublime ode to the Supreme, which has no equal outside of the Book of Books. On leaving the Lyceum, in 1817, he was attached to the Ministry of Foreign Affairs. While in this honorable position, he published his first poems, which immediately attained a high degree of popularity. He now became a traveller, visiting all the romantic sections of the great empire. His principal poetic work, *Eugenii (sic) Oneigin*, is said to be the fullest and most complete imbodiment *(sic)* that exists in Russian literature of the nationality of the country. His small poems and brief stories or novelettes were published in small volumes in rapid succession. His tragedy of *Boris Godunoff* is spoken of by the writer in Blackwood, whom we have quoted, as belonging to the highest order of dramatic literature. He had just finished his History of Peter the Great, when he became involved in the quarrel which resulted in his death, at the age of thirty-eight.

He was not ashamed of his negro ancestor. On the contrary, he seems to have been proud of his descent. He has consecrated more than one of his smaller poems to the memory of the black sea captain; and his works contain frequent allusions to his African blood.

We have alluded to this remarkable man for the purpose of exposing the utter folly and injustice of the common prejudice against the colored race in this country. It is a prejudice wholly incompatible with enlightened republicanism and true Christianity. It degrades the possessor as well as its victim. With our feet on the neck of the black man, we have taunted him with his inferiority, shutting him out from school and college, we have denied his capacity for intellectual progress; spurning him from the meeting-house and church communion, we have reproached him as vicious, as incapable of moral elevation. What is this, in fact, but the common subterfuge of tyranny, seeking an excuse for its

119

oppression by maligning its unhappy objects, and making the consequences of its own cruelty upon them an apology for its continuance? With such examples of the intellectual capacity of the colored man as are afforded by L'Overture and Petion, of Hayti: Dumas, of France; Pushkin, of Russia; and Placido, the slave poet and martyr of Cuba, to say nothing of such men as James McCane Smith, Frederick Douglass, Henry H. Garnett, and Henry Bibb, in our own country; it is scarcely in good taste for white mediocrity to taunt the colored man with natural inferiority. Do not Toussaint's deeds for freedom, and Pushkin's songs of a great nation, waken within all hearts the sympathies of common nature?

> "There spoke our brother! There our father's grave
> Did utter forth a voice!"

In the colored man's follies and crimes, his loves and hatreds, his virtues and weaknesses, we recognize our common humanity, and realize the truth of the inspired Apostle's language—"God hath made of one blood all the Generations of men."

J. G. W.

National Era, Washington, February 11, 1847.

THE POETRY OF HEART AND HOME

(William H. Burleigh)

The great charm of Scottish poetry consists in its simplicity, and genuine, unaffected sympathy with the common joys and sorrows of daily life. It is a home-taught, household melody. It calls to mind the pastoral bleat on the hillsides, the kirk bells of a summer Sabbath, the song of the lark in the sunrise, the cry of quail in the corn land, the low of cattle, and the blithe carol of milkmaids "when the rye comes hame" at gloaming. Meetings at fair and market, blushing betrothments, merry weddings, the joy of

120

young maternity, the lights and shadows of domestic life, its bereavements and partings, its chances and changes, its holy deathbeds, and funerals solemnly beautiful in its quiet kirkyards — these furnish the hints of the immortal melodies of Burns, the sweet ballads of the Ettrick Shepherd and Allan Cunningham, and the pathetic lays of Motherwell. It is the poetry of Home, of Nature and the Affections. All this is sadly wanting in our young literature. We have no songs; American domestic life has never been hallowed and beautified by the sweet and graceful and tender associations of poetry. We have no Yankee pastorals. Our rivers and streams turn mills and float rafts, and are otherwise as commendably useful as those of Scotland; but no quaint ballad, or simple song, reminds us that men and women have loved, met, and parted, on their banks, or that beneath each roof within their valleys the tragedy and comedy of life has been enacted. Poetry is not one of our household gods. A single glance at those great, unshapely, shingle structures, glaring with windows, which deform our landscapes, is sufficient to show that they have not been reared by the spell of pastoral harmonies, as the walls of Thebes rose at the sound of the lyre of Amphion. Our poetry is cold — abstract — imitative — the labor of overtasked and jaded intellects, rather than the spontaneous out-gushing of hearts warm with love, and strongly sympathizing with human nature as it actually exists about us — with the joys and griefs, the good and even the ill of our common humanity. Exceptions, of course, may be made, as in the case of Hoffman's fine songs, some of Brainard's poems, and two or three simple and touching home pictures by WILLIAM H. BURLEIGH.

The poetry of the latter gentleman is by no means so well known as it deserves to be. More ambitious, although in many instances far less meritorious, writers claim the ear of the public. His intimate connection for several years with an unpopular cause has not been favorable to his literary reputation — the poet has been lost in the earnest and active abolitionist. Our readers, we are persuaded, will thank us for reviving such lines as the following:

"Deem not, beloved, that the glow
Of love with youth will know decay;

121

For, though the wing of time may throw
    Its shadows o'er our way,
The sunshine of a cloudless faith,
    The calmness of a holy trust,
Shall linger in our hearts till Death
    Consigns their dust to dust.

The earnest passion of our youth,
    The fervor of affection's kiss,
Love, born of purity and truth —
    All pleasant memories —
These still are ours while looking back
    Upon the past with moistened eyes,
Oh, dearest! — on our life's brief track
    How much of sunshine lies!

Men call us poor — it may be true —
    Amidst the gay and glittering crowd
We feel it, though our wants are few,
    Yet envy not the proud.
The freshness of love's early flowers,
    Heart-sheltered through long years of want,
Pure hopes and quiet joys, are ours,
    Which wealth could never grant.

Something of beauty from thy brow,
    Of lightness from thy household tread,
Hath passed; but thou art dearer now
    Than when our vows were said.
A softer beauty round thee beams,
    Chastened by time, yet calmly bright;
And from thine eye of hazel beams
    A deeper, tenderer light.

The mother, with her dewy eye,
    Is dearer than the blushing bride
Who stood, three happy years gone by,
    In beauty by my side!
OUR FATHER, throned in light above,

122

Hath blest us with a fairy child,
A bright link in the chain of love —
    The pure and undefiled!

Rich in the heart's best treasure, still
    With a calm trust we'll journey on,
Linked heart with heart, dear wife! until
    Life's pilgrimage be done.
Youth, beauty, passion — these will pass,
    Like everything of earth, away —
The breath-stains on the polished glass
    Less transient are than they.

But love dies not — the child of God —
    The soother of life's many woes —
She scatters fragrance round the sod
    Where buried hopes repose!
She leads us with her radiant hand
    Earth's pleasant streams and pastures by,
Still pointing to a better land
    Of bliss beyond the sky!"

The death of a child is a trite subject; but the following lines
will not fail to commend themselves to the hearts of all bereaved
ones, as both beautiful and true:

"OUR BESSIE.

Our Bessie was as sweet a girl
    As ever happy mother kissed,
And when our Father called her home,
    How sadly was she missed.
For, grave or gay, or well or ill,
    She had her thousand winning ways,
And mingled youthful innocence
    With all her tasks and plays.

How softly beamed her happy smile,
  Which played around the sweetest mouth
That ever fashioned infant words;
  The sunshine of the South,
Mellowed and soft, was in her eye,
  And brightened through her golden hair;
And all that lived and loved, I ween,
  Did her affection share.

With reverent voice she breathed her prayer,
  With gentlest tones she sung her hymn;
And when she talked of heaven, our eyes
  With tears of joy were dim.
Yet in our selfish grief we wept,
  When last her lips upon us smiled;
Oh! could we, when our Father called,
  Detain the happy child?

Our home is poor, and cold our clime,
  And misery mingles with our mirth;
'Twas meet our Bessie should depart
  From such a weary earth.
Oh! she is safe — no cloud can dim
  The brightness of her ransomed soul;
Nor trials vex nor tempter lure
  Her spirit from its goal.

We wrapt her in her snow-white shroud,
  And crossed, with sadly tender care,
Her little hands upon her breast,
  And smoothed her sunny hair.
We kissed her cheek, and kissed her brow,
  And if aright we read the smile
That lingered on the dear one's lips,
  It told of heaven the while!"

Those of our Southern readers who have supposed that an abolitionist must necessarily be a sour-featured fanatic, prompted by envy and malice to disturb their quiet, and excite their slaves to rebellion and massacre, would, we think, be speedily undeceived by an acquaintance with the life and character of such men as the author of the foregoing lines. The same warm affections and deep and tender sympathies which breathe in his writings, prompted him early in life to devote his best energies to the cause of universal freedom. His habits and literary taste, no less than his wordly interest, inclined him to a more quiet sphere, but his choice seems to have been made in accordance with the sentiment of one of his sonnets:

" 'Like thee, oh stream to glide in solitude
Noiselessly on, reflecting sun or star,
Unseen by man, and from the great world's jar
Kept evermore aloof — methinks 'twere good
To live thus lonely through the silent lapse
Of my appointed time.' Not wisely said,
Unthinking Quietist! The brook hath sped
Its courses for ages through the narrow gaps
Of rifted hills and o'er the reedy plain,
Or 'mid the eternal forests, not in vain —
The grass more greenly groweth on its brink,
And lovelier flowers and richer fruits are there,
And of its crystal waters myriads drink,
That else would faint beneath the torrid air."

He is yet a young man, and it is to be hoped that he will do much to give a healthier spirit and a more natural tone to our literature. His power lies in his truthfulness, simple pathos, and hearty sympathy with home-felt joys and sorrows:

— "The music to whose tone
The Common pulse of man keeps time."

J. G. W.

National Era, Washington, September 9, 1847.

Some sentences from this were used by Whittier as introductory material for the essay "Robert Dinsmore," *The Prose Works of John Greenleaf Whittier,* Boston, 1892, II, 245-260.

MACAULEY'S* REJECTiON AT EDINBURGH

The late election of members of Parliament in Great Britain has been characterized by many extraordinary results, not the least remarkable of which is the rejection of Thomas Babington Macauley, by his Edinburgh constituency, and the election of an obscure individual, 'one Mr. Cowan,' over the most brilliant Essayist of the age, holding a high place in Her Majesty's government, and one of the best orators of the Whigs in the House of Commons. The leading Whig prints, as might be expected, denounce the electors of Edinburgh in no measured terms. The London press is especially loud in its complaints, maintaining that, by rejecting a world-famous orator and writer, who was only guilty of habitually and scornfully misrepresenting their principles, and electing in his place a sober, kirk-going trader, who is of their own way of thinking, the citizens of the modern Athens have covered themselves with disgrace, paralleled only by the people of ancient Athens in banishing Aristides.

The truth of the matter seems to be, that the brilliant Essayist, like too many other men of genius, of whom history takes note, has been more than suspected of prostituting his fine talents and readiness of tongue and pen in the service of Power against Right. He has been the literary slave of the Whigs—a party once the embodiment of Reform in Great Britain, now disavowing its early liberalism, and, if not actually travelling backward, making at least a dead stand. As a politician, he is what Bacon and Burke were in their day—the protege of the aristocracy, not the tribune of the people. The Whig party, of which he is a placeman, has not kept pace with the popular feeling against ecclesiastical rulers and church endowments. When a large public meeting, representing the Dissenters of Great Britain, remonstrated against the grant to Maymouth College, not on the ground of anti-Catholicism, but of opposition to ecclesiastical bribes and endowments, whether bestowed on Popery or Methodism, Macauley held up the

* Misspelling Macaulay's name consistently throughout this essay, Whittier seems to have had no trouble with it elsewhere.

remonstrants to ridicule in the House of Commons. 'Exeter Hall has had its bray,' said the sarcastic orator. On the state Education Bill, involving the same principle of Church and State connection, he treated the memorials of his constitutents with downright contempt, He seemed to suppose that his popularity as a reviewer and splendid dialectician, conferred so high an honor upon his Edinburgh constituents, that for the sake of retaining it, they would consent to see their petitions and remonstrances trodden under the heel of their representative: that the brilliance of the epigrammatist would atone for the sins of the politician. So, however, the good people of Edinburgh did not reason, with Macauley, as reviewer, they were quite well satisfied; but, as Free Churchmen and Liberals, they demurred to Macauley the placeman. The worthy burghers were not quite ready to follow their eloquent member in his progress towards what they regarded as political perdition, however the broad way thither might be overhung with the choice flowers of his rhetoric. To the horror and indignation of all who suppose genius to be an excuse for any degree of moral and political delinquency, they took counsel of common sense, and rejected their brilliant man of literature, and made choice of a less distinguished but safer representative.

The fate of Macauley at Edinburgh may be found a very useful lesson to the political literati of the United States as well as Great Britain. The day is passing rapidly by wherein thrift follows fawning on genius at the footstool of power. The poet or orator who sells his gifts to the service of oppression in any form, whether that of Church and State union in Great Britain, or of slavery in the United States, must not look much longer for favor from the people. The aspiration of the age is towards Liberty; thither all earnest minds and hearts are tending; and they will not turn aside for the sake of sparing popular geniuses, whose ambition may lead them to block up the pathway of Reform with the tropes and figures of rhetoric.

We have at this moment, in our mind's eye, an American author, who, in one important department of literature, stands confessedly without a rival among his countrymen, whose political course reminds us forcibly of that of the late M. P. for Edinburgh. Like the latter, he, too, in an unlucky moment of ambitious temptation,

'narrowed his mind,

127

And to party gave up what was meant for mankind.'

Instead of exerting his influence to save the party of his choice
from the disgrace and infamy of extending the curse of human
slavery by the annexation of Texas, he aided with pen and tongue
the mighty mischief, and deliberately gave the lie to his early
professions of sympathy with the oppressed, and of inextinguish-
able hatred of slavery. Like Macauley, he has had his reward. He
holds the important office of representative of our government at
the British Court; but should he have occasion, like the former,
to appeal directly with the people, he will learn, with him, that by
putting his literary reputation in the market, and selling for power
and place the admiration bestowed upon his gifts and scholarship,
he has well nigh forfeited, as a politician, the respect and esteem heretofore so liberally accorded to the man.

J. G. W.

National Era, Washington, September 16, 1847

LAMARTINE'S HISTORY OF THE

GIRONDINS, I

The first volume of this work, which has excited so much interest in France, is before us. As might have been expected from
the imaginative and sentimental author of the "Pilgrimage to the
Holy Land," it is a sort of prose poem — the sober muse of History giving place to her sisters of tragic song and rhetoric. The
style is rich and flowing. It lacks, indeed, the sharp outlines of
Thiers, and the strong Rembrandt contrast of light and shade
which lends such terrible distinctness to the pictures of Carlyle;
but it is more elaborately wrought up — a warmer coloring of
romance plays over it. A great deal of artistic skill is manifested
in the delineation of character, and in the biographical sketches,
with which the work abounds. Every way, it is a readable book.

The "History of the Girondins!" No finer subject for the historic pencil could be selected. Amidst the sunshine and gloom — through the joy and terror of the French Revolution, the extravagance, the fanaticism, the brutal licence of a nation which had suddenly cast off the chains of centuries of tyranny, the butcher-work of mob and guillotine, the destruction and re-creation of a social world, — more in their Senatorial robes the young enthusiasts of Southern France, — Vergriand startling King and Kaiser with the inspired eloquence of Freedom, — daring and fiery-souled Louret, breaking the silence of the awe-stricken deputies of France, over whom had hissed from the lips of Robespierre the sinister challenge, "Who dares rise here and accuse me?" with his prompt defiance, " I Robespierre, I Jean Baptiste Louret, accuse thee!" — Barbarous, beautiful as Antinous, answering the death-shots of the King's Swiss with the stormy hymn of his own Marseillais,— the tender soul of Buzet, dreaming of love and quiet and rural happiness amidst the mad turmoil about him, — hear Gaudet, with his trenchant wit and withering sarcasm, — Brissot, with his restless energies and far-reaching schemes, hastening from the Senatorial Hall or the Club of the Jacobins to the home of contented poverty, and to the young wife, who, poor and humble, repaid with fondest devotion the love of her husband; — and, amidst them, one serene and glorious as an angel, gracefulest of the graceful woman — Rood of France, with her flowing dark locks and queenly figure, her deep blue eyes turning tenderly on the dreamy face of Buzet, or reverently upon the calm and thought-worn countenance of her husband, infusing the warmth of her own passionate heart with the cold philosophy of Roland. To follow out the fortunes of this remarkable group — to trace them from their homes in the old Phenician marts, or amidst the vine-yards of the sunny South, through the wild and troubled scenes of Revolutionary Paris, to the scaffold, or the bitterness of exile, has been the single aim of the writer under consideration. His labor is an intermediate one between history and memoirs, dealing rather with men than events.

Our limits will not admit of such a review as would do justice to this book. No impartial and well-informed reader can fail to note many inaccuracies in its details of events and delineations of character; the rigid moralist, measuring all human action by

129

standard of absolute right, will be compelled to take decided exceptions to the judgment which its author passes upon men and events. Few will follow him in his admiration of Robespierre, although his over-estimation may be justly opposed to the indiscriminating odium with which that strange product of the Revolution has been loaded for half a century. The sincerity and earnestness of Robespierre cannot be questioned. His aim was high and noble, but he lacked faith in his fellow-men. Flattery on the one hand, and abuse on the other, made him an egotist. He fancied that he was the Revolution, just as Louis XIV did that he was the State. Hence he struck down all who doubted his infallibility, or refused to see in him the personification of all the virtues, justifying his severity by the belief that enmity to him was treason against liberty.

The sketches of Madame Roland, and of the brilliant group of which she was the centre — of Gustavus of Sweden, Dumouriez, Philip of Orleans, and Danton, are finely drawn. A tragic interest attaches to the story of the brown-locked and peerlessly beautiful Gheroigne de Mericourt — the impure Joan d'Arc of the Parisian populace — fearfully sinned against and sinning—selling her charms to aristocratic voluptuaries, and casting their purchase money, with rigid self-denial, into the treasury of the Republic; avenging her early wrong at the hand of a nobleman of her native province, by leading the squalid victims of vice and poverty into the halls of luxury and titled magnificence, and by demanding from the tribune of the Cordelier's Club the extermination of the aristocracy, by the hands of Danton and his assassins of September. A courtezan, loathing the shame of her condition, she sought solace in dreams of universal freedom and happiness, and appeased the wild unrest of her spirit by active participation in the fierce commotions of the capital. When, too late, she endeavored to moderate the tempest she had aided in raising, and strove earnestly and generously to prevent the shedding of blood, she was seized by the mad populace, her dress torn off, while wretches of her own sex scourged her through the streets. The shame and horror of this scene made her a maniac; and, after miserable years of suffering, she died in a mad-house. Alas, the wages of sin in her case were more than death! How terrible was the guilt of him who turned her young feet from the path of innocence, and transformed the bright angel of a loving household into a fiend, luring others with her strange beauty to the perdition into which she had fallen!

The story of the young Haytian Revolutionist, Oge, is briefly told, with a due appreciation of the heroic character of this remarkable man. Oge had been deputed, with five others, as representatives of the free colored inhabitants of Hayti, to the National Assembly. Descended from slaves, the free colored class were denied the rights of citizens, and oppressed and ill treated by the whites. Clarkson met them at the house of Lafayette the next day after their arrival. He describes them as young men of swarthy complexion, dressed in the uniform of the National Guards; one of them wore the cross of St. Louis. They were well-informed, and solid and sober in their demeanor. On learning the benevolent errand of the English philanthropist, they avowed their hearty hatred of the slave trade, and an immediate amelioration of slavery also, with a view to its total suppression in fifteen years. It should be recollected, that numbers of the free colored class were land proprietors and slave holders themselves.

Admitted to the bar of the National Assembly, the President of that body bade them take courage, for no distinction was henceforth to be drawn between the black and the white man. The white colonists in Paris took alarm; they exerted all their influence to defeat the object of the Haytian deputation; week after week passed, and the latter could obtain no hearing. They began to despair of making head against the intrigues of their enemies. "I begin," said young Oge to Clarkson, "not to care whether the National Assembly admits us or not. But let them beware. We will not be held in degradation. If we are forced to desperate measures, *it will be in vain that thousands will be sent across the Atlantic to bring us back to our former state.*" This was unwitting prophecy.

The last interview which Clarkson held with these young men was deeply affecting. Oge was on the eve of returning to Hayti. Weary, despairing, indignant. The National Assembly had coolly pocketed their contribution of six millions of livres, and had then refused them a hearing. In vain the excellent Englishman implored them to exercise patience. They sadly but firmly replied, that they could endure no more; that the time for forbearance had passed; and, while thanking him for his advice, declared that they felt unable to act upon it. "One of them," says Clarkson, "gave me a trinket by which I might remember him; and, as for himself, he said he should never forget one who had taken such deep interest in his mother Africa." Oge came to Europe only to assert the rights of the free mulattoes; but, influenced by the sentiments of Brissot and Clarkson, he left it the devoted advocate of the entire emancipation of all classes in his native island. On reaching Hayti, he found the white proprietors more hostile than ever to the political rights of mulattoes and freedom of the blacks. They contemptuously refused to carry into effect the law of the Constituent Assembly of the 15th of 5th mo., 1791, admitting those born of free parents to the rights of citizens. Under some of the forms of legality, Oge at last raised the standard of revolution. He demanded of M. Blanchelaude, the Governor of the colony, the promulgation of the decree in favor of his brethren. He put himself at the head of two-hundred mulattoes; his own slaves took up arms for their master and themselves. The Governor's answer to his demand was an armed force to subdue him. A conflict took place, in which Oge was victorious. But a larger force followed, and, after a desperate struggle, the mulatto insurgents were defeated and dispersed. Oge was made captive, and confined in prison at the Cape. His trial was protracted for two months, in order to afford time to ascertain and cut asunder all the threads of the conspiracy. He was finally condemned to death for a crime which, in the mother country, had constituted the glory of Mirabeau and Lafayette.

Impetuous, inconsiderate, and impatient, in his brief struggle with the oppressors of his race, his last days manifested a calm heroism scarcely paralleled in history. His death has all the sublimity of martyrdom. He was barbarously put to the torture in his dungeon. Tormented to the last extremity, he refused to implicate his associates. "Give up all hope," said he to the executioners, "of hearing from me the names of my accomplices. My accomplices are everywhere where the heart of man is raised against the oppressors of men." From that moment, until he was lead out to his execution, he uttered but two words, *"Liberty, Equality!"* When his sentence was read to him, condemning him to the horrible and lingering death of the vilest criminals, he exclaimed, indignantly, "What! do you confound me with criminals, because I have desired to restore to my fellow creatures the rights of man which I feel in myself? Well, you have my blood, but an avenger will arise from it!" He was broken alive upon the wheel. Who can reflect upon his fate without the same emotion which that of Russell and Sidney awakens!—

> Does not the soul to Heaven allied,
> Feel the full heart as greatly swelled,
> As when the Roman Cato died,
> Or when the Grecian victim fell!

The avenger predicted by Oge was not slow in executing his terrible commission. In one night, fifty thousand armed blacks were in rebellion. Eight hundred farm houses and stately mansions blazed at once—the blood of Oge had found tongues of fire.

When the news of Oge's death reached France, the Abbe Gregoire ascended the tribune of the Assembly, with the emphatic declaration, "If Oge be guilty, so are we all. If he who proclaimed freedom for his brothers perished justly on the scaffold, then should all Frenchmen mount there also." Brissot demanded the arrest of Governor Blanchelaude. "Frenchmen of the 14th of July!" he exclaimed, "you are guilty, if the people of color are not innocent!"

We had intended to notice some other portions of the History before us, but as our article has already extended to a greater length than is desirable for our crowded sheet, we leave them until we have found leisure to examine the two remaining volumes. The work is published by Harper Brothers.

J. G. W.

The National Era, Washington, November 4, 1847.

133

LAMARTINE'S HISTORY OF THE
GIRONDINS, II

The second volume of this work has made its appearance, from the press of Harpers. The interest of the story deepens as it proceeds. The characters brought into notice in the first volume are presented in bolder colors, rising in some instances to tragic sublimity, awakening by turns emotions of disgust and pity, hatred and admiration. The sentimental philanthropy and peace-loving philosophy of Robespierre the Deputy, rebuked and thwarted by the enemies of the Revolution, gives place to the bitterness, jealousy, and intolerance of Robespierre the Dictator. Danton emerges from the obscurity of a dissolute and needy law advocate, and becomes the Mirabeau of the populace, urges on the attack upon the Tuilleries of the 10th of August, mounting to the chair of Minister of Justice, to use his own words, through the breach made by the Marseillais cannon. Marat, the lean, mad anchorite, leaves his damp underground cell, and enters the tribune of the Convention, to plead earnestly, almost pathetically, for blood—more blood. The falling fortunes of the Royal family—the imbecility and irresolution of the King—the fiery spirit and energy of the Queen—the war of the two rival factions in the convention—resulting in the execution of the King and the overthrow of the Girondins—are sketched with a vigorous hand. The pictures are life-like.

The volume opens with the arrival of the Marseillais battalion in Paris. The attack on the King's palace and the downfall of the Monarchy follows. In illustration of the fanaticism of the time, the historian states that, for the purpose of furnishing a pretext to the people for rising against the Court, Grangeneuve, a Girondin deputy, actually urged Chabot, one of his colleagues, to murder him, and lay the crime at the door of the aristocrats. (Two quoted paragraphs describing this incident follow.)

134

The insurrection of the 10th of August is described with dramatic effect. The September massacres follow—a dreadful epoch in
the Revolutionary History. Danton, a man with a great deal of
natural humanity, appears to have concerted this wholesale
slaughter, as the only means of preventing a counter revolution,
the extermination of himself and his friends, and the return of the
tyranny which France had thrown off. Even the assassins employed in that terrible crime seem to have supposed that they
were saving their country by exterminating the enemies of Liberty
—doing, in short, at home, what their brethren of the armies were
doing on the frontiers. (Long quotation illustrates these statements.)

. . . .

Danton, the master-spirit of this dreadful out-break, clearly
foresaw the odium which it was calculated to bring upon him, and
met it as one of the necessities of the time, as a sacrifice demanded by patriotism. He had persuaded himself that domestic
treason and foreign invasion should be crushed at once, struck
down by the same terrible band, without pity and without favor.
With the same voice he summoned Paris to break through the girdle of steel and fire which the Duke of Brunswick was drawing
around the revolutionary city, and called upon her to rush the
aristocrats and priests who plotted treason in her midst. Let men
call it what they might, murder or wild justice, the thing was to
be done, and Danton was ready to take the responsibility of its
execution. 'Reputation!' said he; 'what is the reputation of this
man or that? *Let my name be blighted, but let France be free!*'
There is a Satanic sublimity in this sacrifice—this laying of conscience, self-respect, and honorable fame, on the altar of public
weal. Here was a man willing to make himself infamous—to burden his soul with crime—to stamp murder on the forehead of his
memory for all time— in obedience to what he regarded as the dic-
tate of patriotism. We can scarcely see how those who adopt the
atrocious maxim, 'Our country, right or wrong,' can censure him.
Is there anything dreadful, after all, in the massacre of venerable
priests, high-born nobles, and beautiful women, in the prisons of
Paris, than in the slaughter of women and children in the bom-

bardment of Vera Cruz? Does not every poor soldier, who bleeds away his life on the ghàstly battlefields of our Christian civilization, suffer as much as the Bishops and Princes who fell under the daggers of the Parisian mob? In the view of Him who seeth not as man seeth, who holds all men immediately accountable to Him, whether they act alone or with multitudes, whether they act upon the impulse of their own will or that of others, it may well be doubted whether the glorious victories; for which thanksgiving and praise are offered in our Christian temples, are not as hateful as that massacre of September, over which the world has shuddered for half a century. At the very moment when the anti-revolutionary priests and nobles were perishing under the blows of the grim artisans of St. Antoine, eight hundred Prussian soldiers, urged into the territory of France by the Duke of Brunswick, at the instigation of these very priests and nobles, were lying dead on the heights of La Tune and around the mill of Valmy, mangled by shot, and crushed under the heels of horses and the wheels of cannon; and in the neighboring city of Lisle, the groans of women and children, expiring under the blazing ruins of their homes, had succeeded the roar of Prussian artillery and the explosion of shells. 'Let us march against the invaders,' said the populace of Paris; 'but first let us destroy those who have invited them among us.' Danton, at once the leader and minister of that populace, responded to their wishes. Through the whole terrible scene he remained firm. 'These men are guilty,' was his only response to all remonstrances and entreaties. (A column of characterizations and descriptions of the trial of the King under the threats of "ferocious men and unsexed women" concludes the review.)

National Era, Washington, February 17, 1848.

LUCY LARCOM

Some four years since we met, at a meeting of the Improvement Circle of the Factory Girls of Lowell, the author of the following lines ("The Burning Prairie"), who was presented to us as the author of a series of pleasant parables in the *Lowell Offering,* which, in our view, were something more and better than successful imitations of the German writers in this agreeable department of literature. She has since left her loom, and is now, if we mistake not, a school teacher in the West. We thank her for her kindly remembrance of us, and commend her spirited lines to the notice of our readers. That they were written by a young woman whose life has been no long holyday *(sic)* of leisure, but one of toil and privation, does not indeed enhance their intrinsic merit, but it lends them an interest in the eyes of those who like ourselves, long to see the cords of caste broken, and the poor niceties of aristocratic exclusiveness, irrational and unchristian everywhere, but in addition ridiculous in a country like ours, vanish before the true nobility of mind—the self-sustained dignity of a spirit superior to accounting labor degradation, and usefulness a calamity, and which cannot count as common and unclean the duties which God has sanctified.

J. G. W.

National Era, Washington, May 25, 1848.

ON AN ENGLISH CRITIC OF
AMERICAN LETTERS

The Westminster Review, July, 1848. New York: Leonard Scott & Co. For sale by W. Adam, Pennsylvania Avenue, Washington, D.C.

The Edinburgh, Review July, 1848. Published and for sale as above.

Looking over the *Westminster Review,* for July, our attention was arrested by an article, entitled, *Literature of the United States.* It purports to be a review of Griswold's Prose Writers of America, but without pronouncing any opinion respecting the merits of this work, the writer makes it simply a text for some general comments on American Literature. Reviewing, as generally practiced, is rather an *Art* than a *Science*. The writer of the article just mentioned travels over a good deal of ground, and talks quite largely on American Literature, but it is evident that he knows little more about it than the titles of the works Mr. Griswold has seen proper to quote from. What is wanting in knowledge is made up in guesses. He guesses that the philosophy of the Americans must be of the transcendental school; he has heard that Carlyle has more admirers on this side of the Atlantic than in England; he imagines a striking affinity between the American mind and the German. Now, the truth is, the thinkers of this country, if they indulge in the metaphysics of Germany, generally do so for amusement; the majority of them, when in earnest, are very apt to disregard abstract speculations. A little more Idealism would contribute to the elevation of our philosophies and politics.

The reviewer has something to say of the barrenness of this country in history, and yet professes his ignorance of Bancroft's United States! As if an American reviewer should attempt to pronounce judgment on British historical literature, adding, at the same time, that he never read Hume, and could say nothing about him!

He is disappointed with our oratory, but, unfortunately, he seems to have depended alone upon the taste of the elegant Mrs. Maury, for his selections! The readers of her *Statesmen of America* may imagine her taste in oratory, and the judgment of a reviewer who depends upon it.

The other articles in the review are generally highly interesting, their authors appearing to understand their subjects.

The *Edinburgh Review*, for July, is well filled. The article on the Germanic Empire particularly will amply repay a thorough reading.

The French Revolution is discussed in rather a despairing spirit. The reviewer thinks the meager result, secured by the ascendency of the Moderate party in the Assembly, hardly worth the immense outlay of enthusiasm, agony, and blood. We should think so too, were this result final — but this we do not believe.

National Era, Washington, August 24, 1848.

LUCY HOOPER'S POEMS

A new and complete edition of the poetry of the late Lucy Hooper, of Brooklyn, N. Y., has just issued from the New York press. We do but echo the general voice of our contemporaries, when we commend this unpretending and beautiful volume to the attention of our readers. The writer died in 1841, at the early age of twenty-four years, leaving behind her the fragments and occasional pieces which compose it, the delicacy and exquisite tenderness of which are the reflections of a pure and beautiful life. That life, indeed, was itself a psalm of beauty. In the case of many of the gifted children of genius, the moral sense is pained by the discrepancy between their lives and their words; and the heart revolts from the homage which the intellect is compelled to offer. Here, all who knew the writer can only read her poems through the medium of a pleasing and grateful memory of the beautiful and gentle spirit by which they were dictated, and perhaps are liable, in consequence, to over-estimate their merits as literary productions. Yet, in regard to pieces like "Herodias," "Oseola," and others we might name, there can be but one opinion. They are instinct with life, beauty, energy. One of the best poems in the collection was written on the anniversary of the emancipation of the slaves of the British West India Islands. We have seen nothing on either side of the Atlantic, in relation to the glorious event, which equals it in tenderness and pathos. With the simplicity of a child, and the shrinking modesty of a sensitive woman, she did not hesitate to advocate the cause of freedom and humanity, and consecrate youth, beauty, genius to the vindication of unpopular truth; and on the memorable 1st of August, 1838, when the last relic of slavery was abolished in the British islands, being confined to her room by illness, she occupied her time in composing the lines (praised above) which follow.

J. G. W.

National Era, Washington, September 7, 1848.

139

THE SLAVE POET OF
NORTH CAROLINA

Some twenty years ago, a small duodecimo pamphlet was published at Raleigh, North Carolina, containing several short lyrical compositions, by George, a slave of James Horton, of Chatham county, North Carolina. The publication was made by some benevolent citizens of Raleigh, for the purpose of calling attention to the author, and to awaken a feeling in his behalf, which might enable them to fill up a subscription for purchasing his freedom. In the preface they say:

"None will imagine it possible that pieces produced as these have been should be free from blemish in composition or taste. The author is now thirty-two years of age, and has always labored in the field on his master's farm, promiscuously with the few others which Mr. Horton owns, in circumstances of the greatest possible simplicity. His master says he knew nothing of his poetry, but as he heard it from others. George knows how to read, and is now learning to write. All his pieces are written down by others; and his reading, which is done at night, and at the usual intervals allowed to slaves, has been much employed on poetry, such as he could procure—this being the species of composition most interesting to him. It is thought best to print his productions without correction, that the mind of the reader may be in no uncertainty as to the originality and genuineness of every part. We shall conclude this account of George with an assurance that he has been ever a faithful, honest, and industrious slave. That his heart has felt deeply and sensitively in this lowest possible condition of human nature, will easily be believed, and is impressively confirmed by one of his stanzas:

'Come, melting Pity, from afar,
And break this vast enormous bar
   Between a wretch and thee:
Purchase a few short days of time,

140

And bid a vassal soar sublime,
On wings of Liberty.'

Raleigh, July 2, 1829"

The pieces in this little collection indicate genius of no common order. Conned in the midst of the squalid misery and degrading associations of *the slave quarters*, at hours snatched from the interval of rest permitted to the weary field hand, or while working with his comrades in the cornfields of his master, by one who could only, by the pitch light of his cabin fire, with difficulty read the few books which fell into his hands, they certainly merit an honourable place among the "curiosities of Literature." Compared with the earliest productions of the *Ettrick* shepherd, which are in print, they by no means sink in the reader's estimation. Take the following, from the piece on "Creation," as an example (a favourable one, it is true) of the felicity of expression and vigor of thought which characterize the slave poet:

"When each revolving wheel
  Assumed its sphere sublime,
Submissive Earth then heard the peal
  And struck the march of Time!

The march in Heaven begun
  And splendor filled the skies,
And Wisdom bade the morning sun
  With joy from Chaos rise.

The angels heard the tune
  Throughout creation ring;
They seized their golden hoops full soon,
  And touched on every string.

When Time and Space were young,
  The music rolled along—
The morning stars together sang,
  And heaven was drown'd in song."

Is there not something of the divine *afflatus* here manifested? The wind bloweth where it listeth. Something of that inspiration of genius which enabled Haydn to hear the choral harmonies of the "Creation" — the songs of the morning stars, and the rejoicing of the sons of God — seems to have struggled in the breast of the poor negro rhymer. Surely there is a spirit in Man, and the inspiration of the Almighty giveth him understanding. Even in the slave, cast down from the position which God assigned him, herded with beasts, and classed with the wares of the merchant — degraded, abject, and despised — Nature recognizes her lord, although crownless and dethroned, and ministers to him in the organ sounds of the pines which skirt his task-field, in the sunset glory which burns upon his homeward path, and in the stars which shine down upon his humble cabin. It is not even in the power of Slavery to wholly unmake the divinest works of Creation — the Chattel which it lifts upon the auction block is but the mutilated and disfigured image of God.

We copy entire the following poem, not on account of its literary merit, which is far inferior to other pieces in the collection, but because it utters with truthful earnestness the great longing of the author's heart — the cry of a suffering spirit, from its bonds and darkness, for light and liberty:

> *"Alas! and am I born for this,*
> *To wear this slavish chain!*
> *Deprived of all created bliss,*
> *Through hardship, toil, and pain!*
>
> *How long have I in bondage lain,*
> *And languished to be free!*
> *Alas! and must I still complain—*
> *Deprived of liberty!*
>
> *Oh, Heaven! and is there no relief*
> *This side the silent grave—*
> *To soothe the pain—to quell the grief*
> *And anguish of a slave?*

142

Come, Liberty, thou cheerful sound,
　　Roll through my ravished ears!
Come, let my grief in joys be drowned,
　　And drive away my fears.

Say unto foul Oppression, Cease:
　　Ye tyrants, rage no more,
And let the joyful trump of peace
　　Now bid the vassal soar.

Soar on the pinions of that dove
　　Which long has cooed for thee,
And breathed her notes from Afric's grove,
　　The sound of Liberty.

Oh Liberty! thou golden prize,
　　So often sought by blood—
We crave thy golden sun to rise,
　　The gift of nature's God!

Bid Slavery hide her haggard face,
　　And barbarism fly:
I scorn to see the sad disgrace
　　In which enslaved I lie.

Dear Liberty, upon thy breast
　　I languish to respire;
And like the swan unto her nest,
　　I'd to thy smiles retire.

Oh, blest asylum—heavenly balm!
　　Unto thy boughs, I flee—
And in thy shades the storm shall calm
　　With Songs of Liberty."

The following pathetic verses on the death of a young slave
girl, named Rebecca, are worthy of a place with the best productions of the gifted slave poet of Cuba, the martyr of freedom,
Juan Placido. There is something deeply affecting in this dirge

for a slave, by a slave. How bright and beautiful does even the grave seem to him who rejoices that through its portals the spirit of his sister has passed into the glorious liberty of the children of God, where the servant is free from the master, and the wicked cease from troubling!

"I view thee now launched on Eternity's ocean,
    Thy soul, how it smiles as it floats on the wave;
It smiles as if filled with the softest emotion,
    But looks not behind on the frown of the Grave!

The messenger came from afar to relieve thee,
    In this lonesome valley no more shalt thou roam;
Bright seraphs now stand on the banks to receive thee,
    And cry, 'Happy stranger, thou art welcome home!!'

Thou art gone to a feast while thy friends are bewailing,
    Oh, death is a song to the poor, ransomed slave!
Away with bright visions the spirit goes sailing,
    And leaves the frail body to rest in the Grave.

Rebecca is free from the pains of oppression,
    No friends could prevail with her longer to stay;
She smiles on the fields of eternal fruition,
    Whilst Death like a bridegroom attends her away!"

We do not pretend that the verses we have quoted are remarkable either for originality or artistic skill. But, viewed through the medium of the author's condition, they cannot fail to call forth the admiration of the reader. Who can say that the glorious natural gifts of Burns, or Milton, would have shone forth more brightly than that of poor George, if, like him, these world-renowned masters of song had been born the chattel slaves of a Carolina planter!

J. G. W.

National Era, Washington, November 23, 1848

HIRST'S "ENDYMION"

This poem has been long on our table, and we take the opportunity afforded by the termination of the Presidential campaign, to acknowledge the pleasure with which we have read it, at intervals of 'snatched leisure.' We cannot say that we think the author has wisely selected the old and somewhat hackneyed Grecian fable as the subject of so long and elaborate a poem. Keats had already exhausted it. The great merit of the poem, in our view, is the exquisite beauty of some of its descriptive passages. The moonlight really seems to shine over its pictures of lake and river and forest, green vistas and flowing fountains and disporting Naiads. The moon rising over the Grecian mountains--broad, full, and glorious--or, trembling on the western hem of the horizon--Dian's silver bow--as in the ballad of Sir Patrick Spens, the henchman beheld

> "the new moon late yestreen,
> Wi' the auld moon in her arms"--

the slumbering Endymion, with Dian stooping her celestial beauty to his embraces--the picturesque and powerful opening of the third canto, descriptive of "Autumn on the Mountains"--leave us a far more pleasing impression than the love and madness of young Chromia, and the brain-sick follies of Endymion. The beauty of the latter is represented as purely feminine; there is nothing manly about it; and one is constrained to wonder at the bad taste of the coy and fastidious goddess, in tendering to such a delicate and unsexed libel upon manhood the immortality of her celestial favors. The warlike exploits of Endymion are in ill keeping with the girlish softness, which our author describes in his opening canto, with a somewhat ludicrous and particular minuteness. We lack the masculine energy and bearded license of the boar-hunter and leader of Roman legions; we see little in him which earthly woman or celestial goddess would be likely to admire. The old Greek myth itself is true to nature.

We subjoin, as a specimen of the ease and melody of the versification of "Endymion," as well as of its accuracy and beauty of description, the following extract from the opening of the last canto.

(Quotes first seven stanzas.)

The poem is elaborately wrought, and must have cost the author a degree of mental effort to which its theme appears to us by no means commensurate. Life is too short and too earnest to be wasted upon

> — "such stuff
> As dreams are made of, and whose little life
> Is rounded by a sleep."*

J. G. W.

*Note general misquotation by the tired, flurried reviewer.

National Era, Washington, November 30, 1849

POEMS: BY CHARLES G. EASTMAN

We have received from the author this unpretending and modest volume. Many of its best pieces were already furnished to us, and we take a real pleasure in commending them to our readers. Simplicity, ease, and a graceful freedom belonging to the old and pastoral days of New England—something which calls up the memory of the sleighride and the husking—a flavor borrowed of the summer winds blowing over clover bloom, and sweet-briar, or of lilacs nodding before the open window of a moonlight night;—characterize these poems. There is nothing to excite the passions—nothing gloomy or morbid—no mystery—no hints of unutterable things; all is plain, quiet, and genial; the pathos and the mirth, the sunshine and shadow of life, among the corn-growing, sheep-raising yeomanry of the mountains of Vermont. Take the following admirable picture for example:

"The farmer say in his easy chair,
    Smoking his pipe of clay,
And his hale old wife, with busy care,
    Was clearing the dinner away;
A sweet little girl, with fine blue eyes,
On her grandfather's knee was catching flies. (*sic!*)

The old man laid his hand on her head,
    With a tear on his wrinkled face;
He thought how often her mother dead
    Had sat in the self-same place;
As the tear stole down from his half-shut eye,
'Don't smoke,' said the child, 'how it makes you cry.'

The house-dog lay stretched out on the floor
    Where the shady afternoon used to steal;
The busy old wife, by the open door
    Was turning the spinning-wheel;
And the old brass clock on the mantel-tree
Had plodded along to almost three.

Still the farmer sat in his easy chair,
    While close to his heaving breast
The moistened brow and the cheek so fair
    Of his sweet grandchild were pressed;
His head, bent down, on her soft hair lay,
Fast asleep, were they both, that summer day."

Some of the little songs in this collection are note-worthy, for
their artless grace, simple truthfulness, and the entire absence
of meretricious ornament. "Mill May" is a specimen:

"The strawberries grow in the mowing, Mill May,
    And the bob-o'-link sings on the tree;
On the knolls the red clover is growing, Mill May,
    Then come to the meadows with me.
We'll pick the ripe clusters, among the deep grass,

147

On the knolls in the mowing, Mill May,
And the long afternoon together we'll pass
Where the clover is growing, Mill May.

The sun stealing under your bonnet, Mill May,
  Shall kiss a soft glow to your face,
And your lip the red berries leave on it, Mill May,
  A tint that the sea-shell would grace;
Then, come, the ripe clusters among the deep grass
  We'll pick in the mowing, Mill May,
And the long afternoon together we'll pass,
  Where the clover is growing, Mill May!"

Or this:

"She glided down the mazy dance,
  All eyes upon her glancing;
And, everybody vowed, who saw,
  'Twas floating more than dancing.
The bluest eye, the rosiest cheek,
  A lip like morning weather,
When on the flower and grass you have
  The sun and dew together."

We could quote many other passages which have pleased us,
did our limits allow of it; and in dismissing the volume we cannot
but express the hope, which all who read it we are sure will unite
in, that its author will continue, uninfluenced by the dreamy metaphysics, and far-fetched conceits, and shallow philosophies, of
too much of our modern literature, to find subjects for his simple
verse in the scenery of his own hills and valleys, and the home
joys and griefs of human nature, as they exist among his own
people.

                                                    J. G. W.

National Era, Washington, January 25, 1849

NEW BOOKS

(Lowell)

The "Fable for Critics" is understood to be from the pen of James Russell Lowell. It has been welcomed everywhere as a specimen of brilliant and good-natured satire and discriminating criticism. Every page sparkles with wit and humor. The serious and generous soul of the author is however visible through the lambent play of his fancy, a humane heart beats kindly under the light mask of his critical war-dress. The picture of Lydia Maria Child will be recognized by all who have the privilege of her acquaintance. It is as true to life as one of Stewart's portraits. We have marked with italics four lines which contain a strikingly just and beautiful simile: (Quotes 51 lines beginning, "There comes Philothea, her face all aglow," and ending "could they be as Child for one little hour!")

National Era, Washington, February 8, 1849

FIELDS'S POEMS

The Boston Mercantile Association has had the honor of calling forth, on its anniversary occasions, some of the finest metrical productions of New England genius. Sprague's "Curiosity" and Holmes's "Urania" were both delivered at its request; and the largest poem, in the elegant volume before us, was the principal attraction of its last Festival of Reason and Rhyme. A perusal of it in print justifies the applause which its recitation elicited. Its theme is "The Post of Honor," and, in its graceful play and fancy, and depth of feeling and sentiment, it embraces both of the alternatives to which Burns alludes, when he gives to time and chance the direction of his verse —

> "Perhaps it may turn out a song,
> Perhaps turn out a sermon."

The humorous pictures of the office-seeker undergoing the torture of the questioning of the sovereign people, whose votes he solicits, and of the country parson who conceives it to be his duty to obey a "louder call" to the city, are manifestly from real life. As a favorable specimen of the author's more serious manner, we select the following lines, commemorative of the self-sacrifice of Charles Lamb, with whose heroic devotion to his suffering sister the public have but recently been acquainted, the filial love of the poet Gray, and the beautiful charity of the good Sisters of Mercy in Paris:

"The painter's skill life's lineaments may trace,
And stamp the impress of a speaking face;
The chisel's touch may make that marble warm
Which glows with all but breathing manhood's form—
But deeper lines, beyond the sculptor's art,
Are those which write their impress on the heart.

"On Talfourd's page, what bright memorials glow
Of all that's noblest, gentlest, best below!
Thou generous brother, guard of griefs concealed,
Matured by sorrow, deep, but unrevealed,
Let me but claim, for all thy vigils here,
The noiseless tribute to a heart sincere.
Though Dryburgh's walls still hold their sacred dust,
And Stratford's chancel shrines its hallowed trust,
To Elia's grave the pilgrim shall repair,
And hang with love perennial garlands there.

"And thou, great Bard of never-dying name,
Thy filial care outshines the poet's fame;
For who, that wanders by the dust of Gray,
While memory tolls the knell of parting day,
But lingers fondly at the hallowed tomb,
That shrouds a parent in its pensive gloom,
To bless the son who poured that gushing tear,
So warm and earnest, at a mother's bier!

150

"Wreaths for that line which Woman's tribute gave,
'Last at the cross, and earliest at the grave.'
Can I forget, a Pilgrim o'er the sea,
The countless shrines of Woman's charity?
In thy gay capital, bewildering France,
Where Pleasure's shuttle weaves the whirling dance,
Beneath the shelter of St. Mary's dome,
Where pallid suffering seeks and finds a home,
Methinks I see that sainted sister now
Wipe Death's cold dew-drops from an infant's brow;
Can I forget that mild, seraphic grace,
With heaven-eyed Patience meeting in her face?
Ah, sure, if angels leave celestial spheres,
We saw an angel dry a mortal's tears."

The following exquisite little ballad, from the miscellaneous portion of the poems, contains the substance of whole folios of metaphysics and philosophy:

THE TEMPEST

We were crowded in the cabin,
    Not a soul would dare to sleep —
It was midnight on the waters,
    And a storm was on the deep.

'Tis a fearful thing in winter
    To be shattered in the blast,
And to hear the rattling trumpet,
    Thunder, "Cut away the mast!"

So we shuddered there in silence —
    For the stoutest held his breath —
While the hungry sea was roaring,
    And the breakers talked with Death.

As thus we sat in darkness,
    Each one busy in his prayers —

151

"We are lost!" the captain shouted,
    As he staggered down the stairs.

But his little daughter whispered,
    As she took his icy hand,
"Isn't God upon the ocean
    Just the same as on the land?"

Then we kissed the little maiden,
    And we spoke in better cheer,
And we anchored safe in harbor,
    When the morn was shining clear.

The friends of the author—and we know of no one who has more
or warmer, or who better deserves them—will be gratified by the
publication of these pleasant and unambitious passages from the
"snatched leisure" of an active business life. They are characterized by chaste simplicity and healthful sentiment, and reflect the sunny warmth and hopefulness of the heart of the writer.

J. G. W.

National Era, Washington, April 12, 1849

RETRIBUTION:

OR, THE VALE OF SHADOWS

A Tale of Passion

By Emma D.E. Nevitt Southworth

New York: Harper and Brothers

This volume, which first appeared as a serial in the Era, revised and enlarged, forms No. 130 of the Library of Select Novels,

published by the Harpers. The series includes the writings of Bulwer, Bremer, James, Andersen, Jerrold, and Howitt, and other distinguished writers of fiction; but it may well be doubted whether, in terseness of diction, searching analysis of character, intensity of passion, and power of description, any one of them can be regarded as superior to this production of our country-woman. Without being liable to the charge of imitation, "Retribution" reminds us of Jane Eyre, and the later productions of that school. It has their strength and sustained intensity, while it embodies, as they can scarcely be said to do, an important moral lesson. It is well called a Tale of Passion. Painfully intense, its heat scorches as we read. Some of its scenes are overdrawn; mind and heart revolt and protest against those terrific outbursts of passion, on the part of the beautiful fiend, who drags down, in her fatal embrace, the proud, self-deceived statesman. There are a few feeble passages, and some extravagant ones. But, as a whole, we do not hesitate to say, that it is worthy of a place with Brockden Brown's Wieland, Arthur Mervyn, and Edgar Huntley, the only American romances with which we can properly compare it. It cannot fail to be widely read, and we doubt not its success will warrant its author in the entire devotion of her extraordinary powers to a department of literature which, under the influence of a well-principled mind, a generous heart, and healthful sympathies, may be made the medium of teaching lessons of virtue and honor, the Christian duty of self-denial, and heroic devotion to the right and the true, but which has been too often the channel through which impure fancies, stimulants to already over-excited passions, enervating the body and poisoning the soul, have been sent forth on their errands of evil.

National Era. Washington, September 20, 1849.

LITERARY NOTICES*

(E. P. Whipple)

We fear the rather unpromising title of this volume may have the effect to deter a class of readers who hold to the maxim that "words are things," and with whom the word "Lecture" awakens associations of inanity and tediousness, pompous displays of superficial knowledge, oracular utterances of commonplaces, and literary larcenies, in comparison with which hen-roost robbery is reputable; from the pleasure of perusing one of the most brilliant and fascinating volumes which has ever issued from the American press. It consists of six Lectures, or rather Essays, on Authors, in their relation to Life, Novels and Novelists, Wit and Humor, The Ludicrous Side of Life, Genius, Intellectual Health and Disease. In treating these subjects, the author has not inflicted upon his readers a single page of dullness. His style is remarkably direct and energetic, a fitting medium of his clear and sharply defined conceptions—terse, epigrammatic, brilliant, rising at times into true eloquence. But to commend his essays as specimens of fine writing, merely, would do him serious injustice. They are characterized by shrewd insight, practical wisdom, and, as the necessary consequence of the utter absence of cant and sentimentalism, a hearty, healthy tone of sentiment and feeling. His ridicule of the unmanly puerilities of literature, and his contempt for shams, false pretences, affectations and sentimentalisms, remind one of the savage mirth of Longfellow's Northern Jarl, whose

> —"loud laugh of scorn
> From the deep drinking-horn
> Blew the foam lightly."

The concluding Essay on Intellectual Health and Disease touches with no gloved hand the peculiar and besetting sins of

*Lectures on subjects connected with Literature and Life. By Edwin P. Whipple. Boston: Ticknor, Reed, and Fields, 1849.

154

the Northern and Southern sections of our country--the Yankee's conceit and the Southerner's pride. He says of the Yankee, that "he has a spruce, clean, Pecksniffian way of doing a wrong which is inimitable. Believing, after a certain fashion, in justice and retribution, he still thinks that a sly, shrewd, keen, supple gentleman like himself, can dodge, in a quiet way, the moral laws of the universe, without any particular pother being made about it." He illustrates this by the preaching and practice of Yankeedom in respect to the Mexican War. Turning to the South, he says that "the Peculiar Institution" has one vital evil, which would alone ruin any country outside Adam's Paradise—it makes labor disreputable. But it is bad in every respect, corrupting the life both of master and slave; and it will inevitably end, if left to work out its own damnation; in a storm of fire and blood, or in mental and moral sterility and death. "We can," he continues, "sympathize with a person who has had gout transmitted to him as the only legacy of a loving father; but that a man should go deliberately to work, bottle in hand, to establish the gout in his own system, is Quixotic in diabolism. Yet this, or something like this, has been gravely proposed, and some of our Southern brethren have requested us to aid in the ludicrously iniquitous work. No: we should say to these gentlemen, If you have a taste for the ingenuities of mischief, plant, if you will, on your new territory, small-pox, typhus fever, plague, and cholera; but refrain, if not from common honesty, from common intelligence, from planting a moral disease still more destructive, and which will make the world shake with laughter or execration, according as men consider the madness of its folly, or the brazen impudence of its guilt."

We hazard nothing in predicting for these Lectures a wide popularity. They will entitle their author to the same rank as an Essayist, which he already occupies as a Reviewer and critic.

J. G. W.

National Era, Washington, November 1, 1849.

POEMS BY

ALICE AND PHOEBE CAREY

We opened this elegant little book not without some degree of pride in the reflection that we had been one of the first to recognise the rare and delicate gifts of its young authors, and that they had been introduced to the public mainly through the columns of the Era. We miss in this collection some of our favorite pieces, and regret that their places have been filled by others, not so worthy of preservation, whose occasional beauty and felicity of expression are marred by signs of haste and carelessness. Alice Carey occupies the first and largest portion of the book. Her poems evince the imaginative power of the true poet — the divine creative faculty. Her musical instinct is seldom at fault, and there is something peculiarly delicate and graceful in the sweet, half-pensive flow of her verse. Phoebe Carey is a stronger and more vigorous writer — she has less of wild fancy than her sister, but her pieces are on the whole more perfect — she less often sacrifices reason to rhyme, and meaning to melody. "Love at the Grave" is a poem intense with passion. We should be inclined to copy "Our Homestead," "Chalmers," and the sweet little poem entitled "Morning," were it not that the readers of the Era are already familiar with them.

Some of the minor pieces and songs in this collection are remarkable for their harmony and lyrical beauty. We give two stanzas from "The Mill Maid."

> "Each Sabbath time along the aisle
>   Her step more faintly sounded,
> The light grew paler in her smile,
>   Her cheek less softly rounded;
> But never sank we in despair
>   Till with that fearful crying,
> 'The mill maid of the golden hair
>   And lily hand is dying!'

"The mill wheel for a day is still,
The spindle ceased its plying,
The little homestead on the hill
Looks sadder for her dying;
But, ere the third time in the spire
The Sabbath bell is ringing,
Not one of all the village choir
Will miss the mill maid's singing."

The moral tone of these poems is unexceptionable, and in the freest play of their fancy and imagination the writers never lose sight of Christian reverence and humility. We cheerfully commend them and their volume to the public favor.

J. G. W.

National Era, Washington, December 13, 1849.

GREENWOOD LEAVES

A Collection of Sketches and Letters.
By Grace Greenwood.

Some three or four years ago, several exceedingly spirited lyrics appeared in a Western Pennsylvania newspaper. They were not finished productions; they seemed not so much the offspring of deliberate reflection, as of sudden improvisation. There was nothing commonplace about them. They were noticeable for their energy, enthusiasm, beauty, abandonment to the emotions by which they were prompted, and the evidently spontaneous adaptation of language and rhythm to their subjects. Soon after, a series of letters, brilliant, witty, and piquant, appeared in Willis's New York Mirror, under the signature of Grace Greenwood; and we were certainly somewhat surprised to learn that the authorship of these letters, and of the poems which had first attracted our

157

notice, could be traced to one and the same person -- to a young lady, whose home was on the western slope of the Alleghanies. To the letters succeeded a series of tales from the same pen, which have appeared in different periodicals. These last have been widely copied and admired, but, in our view, are by no means the most creditable productions of their writer. Many of them are witty and amusing, but they lack simplicity; there are too many foreign phrases — a trifle too much of good things in the way of love-makings — and the heroes and heroines of some of them are not such as have fallen in the way of our experience, or within the range of our conjectures of the possibilities of what is called fashionable society. The truth is, the writer is not at home in such delineations — for which, let her be devoutly thankful! Let her count it no matter of regret that, to use her own words, she is "not of the ore of which fine ladies are formed; that the atmosphere of the woods and fresh earth is about her; and that, like Macgregor's, her foot is firmest on her native turf."

The volume before us consists of a collection of Prose Sketches and Letters. Among the first, we need not say to the readers of the Era, in which it originally appeared, that the "Rose-wreathed Cross" is a simple, touching, and beautiful story, reminding one of Mackenzie's La Roche. "The Irish Daughter" is full of the pathos of truth in its delineation of the sorrows and loves of a simple emigrant family. The humorous burlesque of "International Copyright," in which some half-score of our American authors appear as complainants against the licensed piracy of publishers on both sides of the Atlantic, is the best thing of the kind we have seen since Horace Smith's "Rejected Addresses." A good caricature is necessarily a recognisable likeness, as it is the exaggeration of well-known peculiarities, and these imitations, so far as manner and language are concerned, are so ludicruously life-like that the friends of the victims cannot fail to "know them at first sight." Longfellow translates from the German of an unpronounceable name, a poem in which the old authors of renown are represented as wailing and wandering on the wrong side of the Styx, and in full view of Elysium, unable to pay Charon for their passage over the river:

"As into solemn silence sinks
Their deep, despairing cry,

158

The first, the last, the only tear
Is brushed from Charon's eye!

He fills his boat with bardic shades,
He turns it from the shore;
And now they pass the Stygian flood,
But work their passage o'er!"

Dr. Holmes gives us "Apollo in America," representing the god in
reduced circumstances, emigrating to the New World, and undertaking the business of author — a poem which would anywhere
pass for genuine. It has the ring of sterling metal.

The "Letters" constitute the best part of the book. In them,
the writer's freedom, freshness, and strong individuality, are fully
developed. All the moods of a versatile and buoyant nature have
free play. She has keen perceptions of the ludicrous, and quick
and earnest sympathies. Humor deepens into pathos; merriment,
.oo hearty, perhaps, for the primness of conventional propriety,
alternates with profoundest sorrow over the wrongs and sufferings
of humanity. Here is a specimen of her humor, from a playful ideal
journey, in which she puts a "girdle round the earth."

I would fain linger on the shores of the Dead Sea, to
search out that record of feminine folly, that memorable
warning to woman-kind, that shining mark of man's reproach, the unfortunate helpmeet of the Patriarch, once
a good wife, undoubtedly, but now chiefly distinguished
for her saline qualities. Perhaps it is a weakness in me,
but I have always had great charity for that woman of the
olden time. Let us reflect how hard it must have gone
with her to leave, with so little warning, all her old
gossips and neighborly cronies; her agreeable city home,
with all the pleasures and conveniences of the metro-
polis, and go vagabondizing off into the rural districts.
And then if she were a good housewife, how hard to
forsake her household comforts, associations, and
duties; the well-filled wardrobe, the granary, the larder;
the cow in the stall, the hen on the nest, the linen in
the loom, the morning cream on the milk! No wonder that
home, love, and womanly regrets, overcame her, and that

159

she turned to take a last fond look, even at the peril of petrifying into a solemn and mournful warning; of becoming a crystallization of her own tears.

There is a vein of drollery and humor in her description of her dog Tom, or "Thomas," as she prefers strangers to call him, which reminds one of some of Lamb's letters to Bernard Barton.

Verily, a dog of pleasant humor and infinite *waggery* is Tom. I took the handsome fellow to have his daguerreotype taken, a few days since. Why, the creature had no taste for the fine arts, or a contempt for this particular branch. It was as though he knew that Rubens and Hogarth and Landseer had *painted* worse looking dogs, and would not be daguerreotyped. Naturally graceful as he is, he managed to throw himself into the most *outre* and ludicrous attitudes, and by his restlessness and awkwardness almost forfeited his good reputation as a setter. He sometimes appeared on the plate with one nose more than even a hunting dog needs for scent; sometimes like those monster lambs exhibited at museums with two heads and two tails. At last, he stretched himself at full length and fell asleep, and we resolved to have him thus taken. Presently his *do*guerreotype was before us. He looked like a Spaniard enjoying his *siesta*. There was the utmost abandon of taking-it-easy comfort in figure, a fine tone of aristocratic repose, but I missed the better standing posture, the animated, up-turned nose, the graceful droop of the ear, and the large, dark, luminous eyes, the life in every limb: in short, it looked like a portrait taken after death, and suggested mournful fancies. To-morrow, we intend making another effort. We think of fastening a tempting piece of meat to the ceiling above, far out of his reach. His eager look of hopeful aspiration will, we think, give a fine effect to the picture. It will seem as though he heard a voice we could not hear — the voice of the hunter Adonis cheering his dogs over the Elysian Fields, or were just about to *set* the Ursa Major.

160

We have only room for a single extract of a widely different character, from the closing letter, describing the *Agnus Dei* of Steinhausen, the German sculptor; the infant Jesus leaning against the cross, with the serpent under its feet.

On the brow of the God-child rests a light, holy and prophetic, whose rays stream backward from the golden days to come. It is not alone the radiance shaken from the wing of the spirit-dove, as he went down into Jordan; not caught from the first adoring look of the unsealed eyes of men born blind. It is not of the sudden morn which broke upon Lazarus's night of death; not of the joy which illumined the desolate home of the widow of Nain; not of the holy hope which shone through the tears of the Magdalene. It is not a gleam of the awful splendors of transfiguration, nor auriole of a triumphant ascension, nor the glory raying off from the crown of martyrs. It is the joy of Heaven over the regeneration of earth; the noontide light of a world's perfect redemption, which bathes the young brow of the world's future Redeemer.

It were well for us to take this serene, prophetic light into our souls, lest, as we look abroad and behold war, oppressions, and innumerable woes, our faith fail us, and we murmur: 'Oh tears of Mont Olivet, oh, blood-drops of Calvary, ye were shed in vain!' — lest the cry of impatient anguish break too often from our lips, 'How long, oh Lord, how long!'

While it is ours 'to labor and to wait,' it is a joy to know that, amid her degradation, her sorrows, and her crimes, earth still cherishes deep in her bruised heart a sweet hope, holy and indestructible, that the day of her redemption draweth nigh; the day foretold by the fire-touched lips of the prophets, the day whose coming was hailed by the martyrs in hosannas which rang through their prison-walls, and went up amid the flames; the day of the fulfilment of the angels' song, the day of the equality taught by Jesus in the temple, on the Mount, and by the wayside, the day of the peace, the rest, and

161

the freedom of God.

We need not say that, like everything from the hands of its publishers, this volume is a neat and elegant specimen of the typographical art.

J. G. W.

National Era, Washington, December 13, 1849.

LONGFELLOW

The Seaside and the Fireside By HWL.

We welcome with real pleasure another volume of poems from the pen of one of the sweetest poets of our time. The pieces in this collection have the careful moulding and patient polish by which art attains the graceful ease and chaste simplicity of nature. There are no rugged lines nor uncouth rhymes, to break the harmony of these felicitous numbers. All whose ears have been tortured by Browning's burlesque of rhythm, should resort at once to the healing influences of "The Seaside and Fireside" melodies of Longfellow.

There are two poems in this little volume which will live, for the common heart of humanity to which they address themselves will not willingly let them die. "The Fire of Drift-wood" shines over some of the dark problems of life, and "Resignation" is full of that tender sympathy and Christian consolation, which, in the language of Scripture, gives "the oil of joy for mourning, and the garment of praise for the spirit of heaviness." A considerable portion of the volume is occupied by a spirited translation of a poem by Jasmin, the Barber-poet of Gascony, which will excite the curiosity of the reader to know more of the author.

National Era, Washington, January 3, 1850.

162

LOWELL'S POEMS

We regret that our Congress-crowded columns will not allow us to notice in a fitting manner this handsome collection of the poems of one of the strongest and manliest of our writers — a republican poet who dares to speak brave words for unpopular truth, and refuses to submit to the inquisitorial expurgation of book-selling caterers to prejudice and oppression. Since his first appearance in public, he has happily overcome a slight tendency to mysticism and metaphysics, and in his later poems he stands out clear and strong in the light of truth and simple nature. He is no longer afraid of the sharp outlines of reality; and so that his thought is fully and forcibly expressed, and his illustration apposite, he seems at times quite careless of the niceties of diction and metaphor. The stamp of the man is on all he does — he is always himself, and none other. He is yet a young man, and, in view of what he has already attained, we have a right to expect a good deal of his future. May he have strength and long life to do for freedom and humanity, and for the true and permanent glory of American literature, all that others less gifted, and subject to less favorable circumstances, have striven in vain to accomplish.

"The Present Crisis" is in our view the noblest poem in the collection. We have read it often, and never without being deeply moved by the magnificent flow of its thought-charged verses. One of the latest-written poems, "Kossuth," is worthy of its name.

"A race of nobles may die out,
    A royal line may leave no heir,
Wise Nature sets no guards about
    Her pewter-plate and wooden ware.

But they fail not, the kinglier breed
    Who starry diadems obtain;
To dungeon, axe, and stake, succeed
    Heirs of the old heroic strain.

The Zeal of Nature never cools,
  Nor is she thwarted of her ends;
When gapped and dulled her cheaper tools,
  Then she a saint and prophet sends.

Lord of the Magyars! though it be
  The tyrant may re-link his chain,
Already strive the victory
  As the just future measures gain.

Thou hast succeeded; thou hast won
  The deathly travail's amplest worth;
A nation's duty thou hast done,
  Giving a hero to our earth!

And he, let come what will of wo,
  Has saved the land he strove to save;
No Cossack hordes, no traitor's blow,
  Can quench the voice shall haunt his grave.

'I Kossuth am; oh Future, thou
  That clear'st the just, and blott'st the vile,
O'er this small dust in reverence bow,
  Remembering what I was erewhile.

I was the chosen trump wherethrough
  Our God sent forth awakening breath;
Come chains, come death, the strain He blew
  Sounds on, outliving chains and death!' "

We are glad to see the announcement of a new volume of poems
by the author, to be published in the early part of the present
season.

J. G. W.

National Era, Washington, January 17, 1850.

THE OPTIMIST*

(H. T. Tuckerman)

Taking for its motto this passage from Richter: "We ought to value little joys more than great ones, the night-gown more than the dress-coat: Plutus's heaps are less worth than his handfuls, and not great but little good haps can make us happy" — this is really one of the sweetest and pleasantest books which has fallen into our hands since we read the hundred pages of Steele, Hazlitt and Leigh Hunt. It consists of a series of gracefully-written essays upon a variety of matters pertaining to daily life and society, all which are discussed in the half-serious, half playful style which befits them, and with the genial humanity, urbanity, and good nature, which are characteristic of the author. It is the book of all others which we would commend to summer tourists and sojourners at watering places, to the invalid, and the over-tasked of mind and body. Its calm, quiet appreciation of the beautiful in common and daily life, its grateful presentation of the compensatory elements of our existence, its catholic sympathies, and delicacy of taste and feeling are well calculated to "minister to a mind diseased" by too much familiarity with stilted heroics, melodramatic literature, and "strong writing." It is a book for the household and the heart, full of pleasant fancies and apt illustrations from the poets, simple, unpretending, and modest; and we think no one can rise from its perusal without a kind thought for its amiable author, and a sense of obligation for a rare and healthful entertainment.

J. G. W.

*The Optimist. By Henry T. Tuckerman. G. P. Putnam, New York. Pp. 273.

National Era, Washington, July 4, 1850.

ELDORADO: ADVENTURES IN THE PATH OF EMPIRE

(Bayard Taylor)

With something of the grateful feeling which prompted the memorable exclamation of Sancho Panza, "Blessings on the man who first invented sleep!" we have laid down these pleasant volumes. Blessings on the man who invented books of travel for the benefit of home idlers! the Marco Polos, the Sir John Mandevilles, and the Ibn Batutas of old time, and their modern disciples and imitators! Nothing in the shape of travel and gossip, by the way, comes amiss to us, from Cook's voyages round the earth to Count De Maistre's journey round his chamber. When the cark and care of daily life and homely duties, and the weary routine of sight and sound, oppress us, what a comfort and refreshing is it to open the charmed pages of the traveller! Our narrow, monotonous horizon breaks away all about us; five minutes suffice to take us quite out of the commonplace and familiar regions of our experience; we are in the Court of the Great Kahn, we are pitching tents under the shadows of the ruined temples of Tadmor, we are sitting on a fallen block of the Pyramids, or a fragment of the broken nose of the Sphynx, dickering with Arab Sheiks, opposing Yankee shrewdness to Ishmaelitish greed and cunning; we are shooting crocodiles on the white Nile, unearthing the winged lions of Ezekiel's vision on the Tigris — watching the night-dance of the Devil-worshippers on their mountains, negotiating with the shrewd penny-turning patriarch of Armenia for a sample from his holy-oil manufactory at Erivan, drinking coffee at Damascus, and sherbet at Constantinople, lunching in the vale of Chaumorng, taking part in a holy *fête* at Rome, and a merry Christmas at Berlin. We look into the happiness of travelling through the eyes of others, and, for the miseries of it, we enjoy *them* exceedingly. Very cool and comfortable are we while read-the poor author's account of his mishaps, hairbreadth escapes, hunger, cold, and nakedness. We take a deal of satisfaction in his moscheto persecutions and night-long battles with sanguinary fleas. The discomforts and grievances of his palate under the ordeal of foreign cooking were a real relish for us. On a hot morning in the tropics, we see him pulling on his stocking with a scorpion in it, and dancing in involuntary joy under the effects of the sting. Let him dance; it is all for our amusement. Let him meet with what he will — robbers, cannibals, jungle-tigers, and rattlesnakes, the more the better — since we know that he will get off alive, and come to regard them so many God-sends in the way of book-making.

The volumes now before us are not only seasonable as respects the world-wide curiosity in regard to California — the new-risen empire on the Pacific — abounding, as they do, in valuable facts and statistics, but they have in a high degree that charm of personal adventure and experience to which we have referred. Bayard Taylor is a born tourist. He has eyes to see, skill to make the most of whatever opens before him under the ever-shifting horizon of the traveller. He takes us along with him, and lets us into the secret of his own hearty enjoyment. Much of what he describes has already become familiar to us from the notes of a thousand gold-seekers, who have sent home such records as they could of their experiences in a strange land. Yet even the well known particulars of the overland route across the Isthmus become novel and full of interest in the narrative of our young tourist. The tropical scenery by day and night on the river, the fandango at Gorgona, and the ride to Panama through the dense dark forest, with death, in the shape of a cholera-stricken emigrant, following at their heels, are in the raciest spirit of story-telling. The steamer from Panama touched at the ancient city of Acapulco, and took in a company of gamblers, who immediately set up their business on deck. At San Diego, the first overland emigrants by the route of the Gila river, who had reached that place a few days before, came on board, lank and brown as the ribbed seasand, their clothes in tatters, their boots replaced with moccasins, small deerskin wallets containing all that was left of the abundant stores with which they started — their hair and beards matted and unshorn, with faces from which the rigid expression of suffering was scarcely relaxed. The tales of their adventures and sufferings the author speaks of as more marvellous than anything he had ever heard or read since his boyish acquaintance with Robinson Crusoe and Ledyard. Some had come by the way of Sante Fe, along the savage Gila hills — some had crossed the Great Desert, and taken the road from El Paso to Sonora — some had passed through Mexico, and, after beating about for months in the Pacific, had run into San Diego and abandoned their vessel — some had landed weary with a seven months' voyage round Cape Horn — while others had wandered on foot from Cape San Lucas to San Diego, over frightful deserts and rugged mountains, a distance of nearly fifteen hundred miles, as they were obliged to travel.

The Gila emigrants spoke with horror of the Great Desert west of the Colorado — a land of drought and desolation — vast salt plains and hills of drifting sand; the trails which they followed sown white with bones of man and beast. Unburied corpses of emigrants and carcasses of mules who had preceded them, making the hot air foul and loathsome. Wo to the weak and faltering in such a journey! They were left alone to die on the burning sands.

On the Sonora route, one of the party fell sick, and rode on behind his companions, unable to keep pace with them for several days, yet always arriving in camp a few hours later. At last he was missing. Four days after, a negro, alone and on foot, came into camp and told them that many miles back a man lying by the the road had begged a little water of him, and urged him to hurry on and bring assistance. The next morning a company of Mexicans came up, and brought word that the man was dying. But his old companions hesitated to go to his relief. The negro thereupon retraced his steps over the desert, and reached the sufferer just as he expired. He lifted him in his arms; the poor fellow strove to speak to his benefactor, and died in the effort. His mule, tied to a cactus, was already dead of hunger at his side. A picture commemorating such a scene, and the heroic humanity of the negro, would better adorn a panel of the Capitol, than any battle-piece which was ever painted.

There is a graphic account of the author's first impressions of San Francisco. "A furious wind was blowing down through a gap in the hills, filling the streets with dust. On every side stood buildings of all kinds, began or half-finished, with canvass sheds open in front and covered with all kinds of signs, in all languages.

Great piles of merchandise were in the open air, for lack of store-houses. The streets were full of people of as diverse and bizarre a character as their dwellings: Yankees of every possible variety, native Californians in serapes and sombreros, Chilians, Sonorians, Kanakas from Hawaii, Chinese with long tails, Malays armed with everlasting creeses, and others, in their bearded and embrowned visages, it was impossible to recognise any especial nationality." "San Francisco by day and night" is the title of one of the best chapters in the book.

Our author made a foot journey to Monterey during the sitting of the Convention which formed the State Constitution. He gives a pleasing account of the refined and polite society of this ancient Californian town; and makes particular mention of Doña Augusta Ximeno, a sister of one of the Californian delegates to the Convention, Don Pablo de la Guerra, as a woman whose nobility of character, native vigor and activity of intellect, and instinctive refinement and winning grace of manner, would have given her a complete supremacy in society, had her lot been cast in Europe or the United States. Her house was the favorite resort of the leading members of the Convention, American and Californian. She was thoroughly versed in Spanish literature, and her remarks on the various authors were just and elegant. She was, besides, a fine rider, and could throw the lariat with skill, and possessed all those bold and daring qualities which are so fas-cinating when softened and made graceful by true feminine delicacy.

He describes the native Californians as physically and morally superior to the Mexicans of other States. They are, as a class, finely built, with fresh, clear complexions. The educated class very generally are and appear well satisfied with the change of affairs, but the majority still look with jealousy on the new-comers, and are not pleased with the new customs and new laws. The Californians in the Convention seemed every way worthy of their position. General Vallejo is a man of middle years, tall, and of commanding presence—with the grave and dignified ex-pression of the old Castilian race. With him were Cavarrubias, the old Secretary of the Government, Pico, Carvillo, Pedrorena, La Guerra, and a half-blood Indian member, Dominguez, who, together with many of the most respectable and wealthy citizens of California, is now excluded from voting by a clause of the Constitution, which denies that privilege to Indians and negroes. This unjust exception—a blot on an otherwise admirable Constitution—was adopted after a warm debate, and against fierce opposition. The attempt to prohibit free people of color from inhabiting the State failed by a large majority. *The clause prohibiting slavery passed by the vote of every member.*

The account of the close of the Convention is sufficiently amusing. The members met and adjourned, after a brief session, and their hall was immediately cleared of forum, seats, and tables, and decorated with pine boughs and oak garlands. At eight in the evening, it was thrown open for a ball. Sixty or seventy ladies, and as many gentlemen, were present. Dark-eyed daughters of Monterey and Los Angeles and Santa Barbara, with Indian and Spanish complexions, contrasted with the fairer bloom of belles from the Atlantic side of the Nevada. There was as great a variety of costume as of complexion. Several American officers were there in their uniform. In one group might be seen Captain Sutter's soldierly moustache and clear blue eye; in another, the erect figure and quiet, dignified bearing of Vallejo. Don Pablo de la Guerra, with his handsome aristocratic features, was the floor manager, and gallantly discharged his office. Conspicuous among the native members, were Don Miguel Pedrorena and Jacinto Rodriguez, both polished and popular gentlemen. Dominguez, the Indian, took no part in the dance, but evidently enjoyed the scene as much as any one present. The most interesting figure was that of the Padre Ramirez, who, in his clerical cassock, looked until a late hour. "If the strongest advocate of priestly decorum had been present," says our author, "he could not have found it in his heart to grudge the good old padre the pleasure which beamed in his honest countenance."

The next day the Convention met for the last time. The parchment sheet, with the engrossed Constitution, was laid upon the table, and the members commenced affixing their names. Then the American colors were run up the flagstaff in front of the Hall, and the guns of the fort responded to the signal. The great work was done. California, so far as it depended on herself, was a State of the great Confederacy. All were excited. Captain Sutter leaped up from his seat, and swung his arm over his head.

170

"Gentlemen!" he cried, "this is the happiest hour of my life. It makes me glad to hear the cannon. This is a great day for California!" Recollecting himself, he sat down, the tears streaming from his eyes. His brother members cheered. As the signing went on, gun followed gun from the fort. At last the *thirty-first* was echoed back from the hills. "That's for California!" shouted a member, and three times three cheers were given by the members. An English vessel caught the enthusiasm, and sent to the breeze the American flag from her mast head. The day was beautiful; all faces looked bright and happy under the glorious sunset. "Were I a believer in omens," writes our tourist on the spot, "I would augur from the tranquil beauty of the evening—from the clear sky and sunset hues of the bay--more than all, from the joyous expression of every face—a glorious and happy career for the "STATE OF CALIFORNIA"!

Our author visited several of the most important "diggings," and his account of their location, productiveness, etc., does not materially differ from the descriptions which have become familiar to all our readers. It is evident from his statements, that with good health and perseverance, any reasonable expectation of wealth on the part of the miners may be realized, in a few months or years, according to the richness of the "diggings," or the ease with which they may be worked. What, however, has interested us more than the gold-product of California, is the confirmation which our traveller gives to the statements of Fremont and King, relative to the richness of its soil, and its great agricultural capacities. The valleys of the Sacramento and San Joaquim alone are capable of supporting a population of two millions, if carefully cultivated. The deep, black, porous soil produces the important cereal grains, although on the seaboard the air is too cool for the ripening of Indian corn. Enormous crops of wheat may be obtained by irrigation, such as was successfully practiced by the great Jesuit missions; and, without it, from forty to fifty bushels to the bushel of seed have been raised. Oats of the kind grown on the Atlantic grow luxuriantly and wild, self-sown on all the hills of the coast, furnishing abundant supplies for horses. Irish potatoes grow to a great size, and all edible roots cultivated in the States are produced in perfection, without irrigation.

171

The climate of San Francisco is unquestionably disagreeable; the cold, fierce winds which sweep over the bay, and they alternating with extreme heats, are prejudicial to health and comfort. Inland, however, in the beautiful valleys of San Jose and Los Angelos, the climate is all that could be desired. The heat during the summer months is indeed great, but its dryness renders it more endurable than the damp sultriness of an Atlantic August. At Los Angelos, latitude 34°7'' long, W. 113°, and forty miles from the ocean, the mean monthly temperature of ten months was as follows: June 73 deg., July 74, August 75, September 75, October 69, November 59, December 60.

Our author describes with a poet's enthusiasm the fine atmospheric effects of the Californian sunsets. Fresh from his travels in Italy, and with the dust of that Pincian hill still on his sandals from whence Claude sketched his sunsets, he declares that his memory of that classic atmosphere seems cold and pale, when he thinks of the splendor of evening on the bay and mountains of San Francisco.

The chapter on "Society in California" may prove of much practical utility, and should be read by all who are smitten with the gold fever. California is no place for the sick, the weak, the self-indulgent, the indolent, the desponding. There must be a willingness to work at anything and everything, and stout muscles to execute the will. Our author estimates that nearly one third of the emigrants are unfitted for their vocation, "miserable, melancholy men, ready to yield up their last breath at any moment, who left home prematurely, and now humbly acknowledge their error." His own happy constitution and buoyant health led him to look on the best side of things, and to take the sunniest possible view of the condition of the new country he was exploring, but occasionally he reveals incidentally the reverse of the picture. Here is a sketch of a sick miner at Sacramento City, which is enough to make even California "gold become dim, and the fine gold changed."

"He was sitting alone on a stone beside the water, with his bare feet purple with cold on the cold, wet sand. He was wrapped from head to foot in a coarse blanket, which shook with the violence of his chill, as if his limbs were about to drop in pieces. He seemed unconscious of all that was passing; his long matted hair hung over his wasted face, his eyes glared steadily forward with an expression so utterly hopeless and wild, that I shuddered at seeing it. This was but one of a number of cases, equally sad and distressing."

The hardy and healthy portion of the emigrants, under the stimulating excitements of the novel circumstances of their situation, seemed to revel in the exuberance of animal spirits. Each seemed to have adopted the rule of the wise man: "Whatsoever thy hand findeth to do, that do with all thy might." They speculated, dug, or gambled, with an almost reckless energy. All old forms of courtesy had given place to hearty, blunt good fellowship in their social intercourse. They reminded our traveller of the Jarls and Norse sea-kings, and in the noisy and almost fierce revelry of these bearded gold-hunters around their mountain fires, he seemed to see the brave and jovial Berseckers of the middle ages.

We cannot forbear quoting a paragraph in relation to the great question of our time, "The Organization of Labor."

"In California, no model phalanxes or national workshops have been necessary. Labor has organized itself, in the best possible way. The dream of attractive industry is realized; all are laborers, and equally respectable; the idler and the gentleman of leisure, to use a phrase of the country 'can't shine in these diggings.' Rich merchandise lies in the open street; and untold wealth in gold dust is protected only by canvass walls, but thefts and robbery are seldom heard of. The rich returns of honest labor render harmless temptations which would prove an overmatch for the average virtue of New England. The cut-purse and pick-pocket in California find their occupation useless, and become chevaliers of industry, in a better sense than the term has ever before admitted of. It will appear natural, says our author, that California should be the most democratic country in the world. The practical equality of all the members of the community, whatever might

173

be the wealth, intelligence, or profession of each, was never before so thoroughly demonstrated. Dress was no gauge of respectability, and no honest occupation, however menial in its character, affects a man's standing. Lawyers, physicians, and ex-professors, dug cellars, drove ox-teams, sawed wood, and carried baggage, while men who had been army privates, sailors, cooks, or day laborers, were at the head of profitable establishments, and not unfrequently assisted in some of the minor details of government. A man who would consider his fellow beneath him on account of his appearance or occupation, would have had some difficulty in living peaceably in California. The security of the country is owing in no small degree to this plain, practical development of what the French reverence as an abstraction, under the name of *Fraternité*. To sum up all in three words, *Labor is respectable.* May it never be otherwise while a grain of gold is left to glitter in Californian soil!''

Our author returned by way of Mazatlan and the city of Mexico, meeting with a pleasant variety of adventures, robbery included, on his route. In taking leave of his volumes, we cannot forbear venturing a suggestion to the author, that he may find a field of travel, less known and quite as interesting at the present time, in the vast Territory of New Mexico–the valley of the Del Norte, with its old Castilian and Aztec monuments and associations; the Great Salt Lake, and the unexplored regions of the great valley of the Colorado, between the mountain ranges of the Sierra Madre and the Sierra Nevada. We know of no one better fitted for such an enterprise, or for whom, judging from the spirit of his California narrative, it would present more attractions.

Eldorado: Adventures in the Path of Empire. By Bayard Taylor. New York. 1850. Two volumes.

National Era, Washington, July 4, 1850

THE MORNING WATCH: A NARRATIVE

This poem—which has faults enough to ruin an ordinary candidate for poetical distinction, and merit enough to atone for still greater—is a sort of religious allegory or representation of the spiritual pilgrimage of life. An aged traveller tells the story of his journey from childhood—his temptations and experiences in the world of sin and death—his escape into a purer atmosphere—and his earnest strivings to reach the far-off land of beauty and peace and holiness, concerning which vague intimations had reached him. As a whole it fails of its intended effect, through lack of distinctness and method, and there is a slip-shod negligence in much of its versification. Its beauty is in detached passages of sentiment or description, where the rhythm flows on softly and musically, with a dreamy yet not unpleasing vagueness, like a prolongation of Coleridge's dream of Kubla Khan. The following passage may serve as an illustration:

"And the crimson moon goes up and on
   Into the azure of the sky
Where in the stillness of the dawn
   Westerly a cloud sails by;
And from the dawn it taketh away
Crimson and white and apple gray,
   Silently, as sails the cloud,
The night-dews rise in wreaths of mist;
   The cataract of the mountains, loud
Calls to the hills, its bright robe gleams
   Silver and gold and amethyst:
And what like muffled thunder seems
   Is the low crumbling rush and roar
   Of breakers on the distant shore.

The air is still: even as a bell
All sweet sounds it cometh well;
But now, as a bell, they seem to say,
All voices near or far away
From the distant hills and mountains gray,
Or the uttermost parts of the sounding sea,
'May God have mercy upon this day!'

Wondering I looked at the sweet Heaven,
That such a prayer must needs be given,
   So bright, I said, so pure and holy
   Doth seem this golden day!
But straightway came the better thought
That 'twas my sin the prayer had wrought;
   The burden of my sin which lay
   Even as a curse upon the day—
   A subtle poison running through
   The white mist and the morning dew."

In the following impressive lines; the healing influences of
nature upon the sin-sick and guilty spirit of the wanderer are
well described:

   "I had no thought of prayer:
   I dared not but to be
   As by the mountains and the sea
   And by the lonely cataract, within
   An atmosphere of peace and love,
   With voices which acceptably above
Go up forever and forever: this to me
Was as my daily food, my breath, my life, and free

   As was the manna in the wilderness, and as one
   Within some lofty nave alone
   Breathes in the music of the choir,
   And with a still wail witnesses
   The Holy Mysteries
   But does not raise
   His voice, or utter one 'Amen,'
   Or in the *'Gloria'* swell the hymn of praise:

   But, kneeling far apart,
   All mute and lone,
   Hears only one deep tone—
The music of a prayer unuttered at his heart—
   Though, but not daring speech—
   'Christ have mercy upon us!'
So by the lonely cataract, on the hill,

And by the mountains and the sea,
I heard the everlasting worship and was still!
At last there came a change, methought that all
The sweet low voices musical,
From falling waters and the evening breeze,
Bound seaward o'er the forest trees,
And from the mountain passes and the sea,
Forever and forever rose for me,
Forever through the still and starry night,
Forever in the sun and in the light,
In storm and tempest and the rocking winds,
Like angels flying o'er
A land accursed, and evermore
Beseeching Heaven, 'Spare, oh spare!'
So rose the universal prayer
Forever and forever rose for me!"

The power of the author, however, may be perhaps better in-
ferred from a passage like the following, describing a vision of
the lost world:

- - - - - - "Suddenly,
Within the sun illuminated space, star strewn,
Monstrous and formless, as though thrown
        From Chaos and the Everlasting night—
Which gave not, nor received, out backward hurled
        Upon the skies the music and the light—
Silent amidst rejoicings, sailed a silent world!
Its light, if such it was, was as the light
        Of breaking waters on a midnight sea,

Where ever storm and darkness and afright
        Mingle perpetually
Its sky, low hung and starless, such as night
And coming tempest flash upon the sight—
A darkness beaded as the sea with foam,
Where slept the lightnings of the wrath to come!

177

Upon this silent world there stood
A vast and countless multitude,
With downward eyes, and lips of bloodless white;
And speechless all—no word of love or hate,
Or fear or agency—no sigh or moan
But, as from some ponderous bell, sky hung,
    Unseen within the vault above,
In pauses from its iron tongue
Fell through the gloom (as 'twere a groan
From all that host) one deep sad tone—
A single toll; at which all eyes were raised
And lips apart each looked a kind of joy—
    Something like madness—but soon again,
As a quick lightning to the brain,
    Upon their downward face fell
    The look of woe unutterable!

A mother and her child met there;
Both were so beautiful and fair,
That, so it seemed, a milder mood
Pervaded that vast multitude.
But the mother gazed at her speechless child,
    And the child looked up at her silent mother,
One with a look so wan and wild,
    And with so blank despair the other;
And prayed (oh, God forgive the sin!)
That Jesus Christ might die again,
Or some quick madness set them free
From such unnatural misery
But still they gazed that child and mother,
    And still with look more terrible;
Till suddenly each spurned the other,
    And then forever on them fell
    (Oh, type and countersign of Hell!)
    That look of woe unutterable!"

There is something in this vividly drawn and terrible picture
which reminds one of Dante's Inferno. We can call to mind few
passages in modern poetry which may so well compare with the
grand and awful fancies of the "dark Italian Hierophant."

The entire poem, pervaded as it is by deep religious feeling and reverence, and evincing on almost every page an enthusiastic love of the beauty and harmony of nature, leaves a pleasing impression of the author, not unconnected with some degree of regret that he did not more carefully elaborate his production, and render it, as a whole, worthy of the praise which portions of it so well merit.

J. G. W.

National Era, Washington, August 22, 1850

LITERARY NOTICES

THE BROKEN BUD, OR REMINISCENCES OF A BEREAVED MOTHER. New York: Carter and Brothers. Pp. 324.

This touching and beautiful tribute of a bereaved mother to the memory of her beloved child owes its origin to the writer's desire to preserve in manuscript for her surviving children a memorial of their departed sister; and it has been published in the hope of affording to other suffering hearts something of the consolation which its preparation gave to her own. Influenced by the earnest desire which, in her grief, she had felt for the sympathy and spiritual communion of those who had tasted with her the bitter cup of bereavement, she has been induced to lift the veil from the sacredness of her sorrows and consolations, and, to use the words of Baxter after the death of his companion, "to become passionate in the view of all."

We have no doubt that the benevolent end of the writer will be fully answered by this graceful and tender tribute of affection. It will commend itself to all who mourn; to the sad sisterhood of sorrow; the unnumbered Rachels weeping for those dear ones who are not.

> "There is no flock, however watched and tended,
>   But one dead lamb is there;
> There is no fire side, howsoe'er defended,
>   But has one vacant chair."

The book is by no means a gloomy one. The shadow of the great bereavement is, indeed, as it must be, deep and dark, but it is preceded by a sweet and sunny history of happy childhood, and softened and limited by the consolations and hopes of the Gospel of Him who laid his hand of blessing on the brows of little children, and proclaimed that "of such is the kingdom of heaven."

HISTORY OF MY PETS. Boston: Ticknor and Co. Pp. 109. For sale by Taylor and Maury, Pennsylvania Avenue, Washington.

The juvenile public, and even those of us who are "children of a larger growth," can scarcely fail to thank the writer of this unique and charming little volume. In connection with the history of her biped and quadruped favorites, Grace Greenwood has given an exceedingly pleasant and amusing autobiography of her childhood, and has thus lent human interest to the story of the lives and fortunes of her brute friends. The portraits of man and beast are sketched with so much life and spirit, their peculiarities and good and evil qualities and characteristics are so well defined, that we question whether Landseer, or Grandville, or the famous old Dutch painter, who was styled "the Raphael of Cats," ever transferred to their canvass more striking likenesses. They remind us of Cowper's description of his pets, and of Jane Porter's address to her kitten. The style is admirable, simple, spirited, and graceful and in our judgment far preferable to that of her more ambitious and studied prose pieces. "Toby, the hawk," is the best of the humorous sketches. "Hector, the Greyhound," and "Robin Redbreast" have a touching pathos which will commend them in an especial manner to young readers, whose sunny hearts, as yet undarkened by actual sorrow, find a luxury in ideal sadness, and, to use the language of Wordsworth —

> "Sad fancies do affect,
> In luxury of disrespect
> To their own prodigal excess
> Of too familiar happiness!"

180

The rapid sale and general popularity of this little contribution to our juvenile literature will, we trust, induce the writer to continue her labors of love in this department. The author of such stirring lyrics as "The Poet of Today," and "Arnold Winkelried," need not fear the charge of puerility and childish weakness in following where Hawthorne and Hans Christian Andersen have led the way.

National Era, Washington, January 30, 1851

POEMS BY WILLIAM ALLINGHAM

From the author's well-written and modest preface, rather than from the book itself, which indicates nothing of the " 'prentice hand," we learn that this is his first publication. He dates from Ballyshannon, Ireland; and if we mistake not, the Green Island will have reason to be proud of him, although, judging from the shrewd, plain, common sense advice of his piece entitled "Justice to Ireland," he is not likely to win favor from the noisier portion of his countrymen. Some of his pieces, "The Wayside Well" in particular, have been copied into American papers, from Dickens's Household Words, where they originally appeared. "The Fairies" is an admirable nursery song, which our juvenile readers would doubtless thank us for, if we could afford space for it. We give a verse or two as a specimen:

> "Up the airy mountain,
>   Down the rushy glen,
> We daren't go a hunting
>   For fear of little men!
> Wee folk, good folk,
>   Trooping all together;
> Green jacket, red cap,
>   Gray cock's feather.
>
> "Down on the rocky shore
>   Some make their home,
> They live on crispy pancakes

181

Of yellow tide foam.
　　Some in the reeds
　　　　Of the Black Mountain Lake,
　　With frogs for their watch-dogs
　　　　All night awake!"

J. G. W.

National Era, Washington, May 1, 1851

POEMS BY W. C. BENNET

We have for some time past watched with interest the progress of the author of this volume, for in some of his earliest pieces we discerned, as we thought, the promise of a successful candidate for literary honor. There is much in this little collection to confirm our first impressions. The author's fancy is bold, rather than delicate: he does not belong to the metaphysical or transcendental school: his inspiration "comes of observation," rather than reverie and mental introversion. The Lines to a Skylark — a dangerous subject to touch after Shelley and the Ettrick Shepherd — have the true lyrical fire. Listen to this burst of gladness and rapture, like the skylark's own, from the clear heaven of morning:

"Up! no white star hath the west;
　　All is morning, all is day;
Earth in trembling light lies blest;
　　Heaven is sunshine — up, away!
Up! the primrose lights the lane;
　　Up! the boughs with gladness ring;
Bent are blue-belled flowers again,
　　Drooped with bees — oh, soar and sing!

"Ah! at last thou beat'st the sun,
　　Leaving low thy nest of love;
Higher, higher, quivering one,
　　Shrillest thou up and up above;
Wheel on wheel the white day through,

182

> Might I thus with ceaseless wing,
> Steep on steep of airy blue,
>   Fling me up, and soar and sing!"

The "Winter Song" has the genial heartiness of a Christmas fireside in old England, and the exaltation and sparkling merriment of a New England sleigh-ride. "The Dress Maker's Thrush" is a sad and touching wail of human suffering, destined, like Hood's "Song of a Shirt" and Elizabeth Barrett's "Cry of the Human," to awaken sympathy for the poor and wrong wherever it is heard. Had the author written nothing beside, the sweet pathos of this little poem would go far to entitle him to an honorable place among the living poets of England.

THE DRESS MAKER'S THRUSH.

Oh! 'tis the brightest morning,
 Out in the laughing street,
That ever the round earth flashed into
 The joy of May to meet!
Floods of more gleaming sunshine
 Never the eye saw rolled
Over pavement and chimney and cold, gray spire,
 That turns in the light to gold;
And yet, as she wearily stitches,
 She hears her caged thrush sing:
Oh, would it never were May, green May,
 It never were bright, bright spring!

Light of the new-born verdure!
 Glory of jocund May!
What gladness is out in leafy lanes!
 What joy in the fields to-day!
What sun-bursts are in the woodlands!
 What blossoms the orchards throng!
The meadows are snowed with daisy stars,
 And the wings are thrilled with song;
And yet, as ever she stitches,
 She hears her caged thrush sing:

183

Oh, would it never were May, green May,
　It never were bright, bright Spring!

Close is the court and darkened
　On which her bare room looks,
Whose only wealth is its walls' one print,
　And its mantle's few old books,
A spare cold bed in the corner,
　Her single worn, worn chair,
And the grate that looks so rusty and dull
　As never a fire were there!
And there, as she stitches and stitches,
　She hears her caged bird sing:
Oh, would it never were May, green May,
　It never were bright, bright, Spring!

Out is the gleaming sunshine!
　Out is the golden air!
In scarce a gleam of the bright May sun
　Can dulled and dim reach there!
In the close, damp air of darkness
　That blanches her cheek to white
Her rounded features sharpen and thin,
　And dulls her once keen sight:
And there, as she sits and stitches,
　She and her caged thrush sing:
Oh, would it never were May, green May,
　It never were bright, bright Spring!

Days that are cloudy and dull,
　Winter, though winter bring
Cold, keen frost to her fireless room,
　Are dearer to her than Spring!
For then on her weary sewing
　Less often her worst thoughts come
Of the pleasant lanes and the country air
　And the wood-paths trod by some;
And so, as she wearily stitches,
　She and her caged bird sing:

Oh, would it never were May, green May,
It never were bright, bright Spring!

The contents of the volume are very unequal. Its more ambitious and studied poems are less to our taste than the lyrics we have referred to.

J. G. W.

National Era, Washington, May 1, 1851.

ALICE CAREY

Recollections of Our Neighborhood in Ohio. — Under this title, we understand that a New York publisher is about to issue a volume of prose tales by our correspondent, Alice Carey, already favorably known for her poetical writings. We do not hesitate to predict for these sketches a wide popularity. They bear the true stamp of genius — simple, natural, truthful — and evince a keen sense of the humor and pathos of the comedy and tragedy of life in the country. We need only refer to such pieces as "Mrs. Troost and Mrs. Hill," "A Reminiscence," "Light and Shade," "The Deacon's Folks," and the opening chapter of "Ill-Starred," in support of this estimate of the writer's power. No one who has ever read it can forget the story of the sad and beautiful Mary Wildermings; its weird fancy, tenderness, and beauty; its touching description of the emotions of a sick and suffering human spirit, and its exquisite rural pictures. The moral tone of Alice Carey's writings is unobjectionable always — if we except, perhaps, an occasional outlook upon life, too sad and deprecating. This tendency, however, is relieved by a vivid perception of the ludicrous and humorous in character, which ever and anon discloses itself against the sober-hued background of her pictures. The readers of the *Era* will, we are persuaded, be pleased to meet in a new dress their old acquaintance, Patty Lee.

J. G. W.

National Era, Washington, October 30, 1851.

185

NEW PUBLICATIONS

(Bayard Taylor and R. H. Stoddard)

We are indebted to Ticknor, Reed and Fields, for "Bayard Taylor's Book of Romances, Lyrics, and Songs," and for R. H. Stoddard's new volume of poetry — the latter containing the fine, imaginative poem of "The Castle in the Air," a happy and rich specimen of aerial architecture, quaint, delicate, and voluptuous, such as the "Bard of the Castle of Indolence" might have enjoyed in his vision

> "Of dreams that flit before the half-closed eye,
> And of gay castles in the clouds that pass
> Forever flashing round a sunset sky."

Some of the minor poems are characterized by a peculiar delicacy of fancy and expression. The following picture of a sea-side scene, on a moonlight night, is worthy of Tennyson:

> "The yellow moon looks slantly down
> Through seaward mists upon the town;
> And, like a mist, the moonshine falls
> Between the dim and shadowy walls.
>
> I see a crowd in every street,
> But cannot hear their falling feet:
> They float like clouds through shade and light,
> And seem a portion of the night.
>
> The ships have lain for ages fled
> Along the waters, dark and dead;
> The dying waters watch no more
> The long black line of spectral shore.
>
> There is no life on land or sea,
> Save in the quiet moon and me;
> Nor ours is true, but only seems,
> Within some dead old world of dreams!"

186

To Bayard Taylor's book we cannot now do justice. As one of the early appreciaters of his rare gifts, we fell an honest pride in his growing reputation, which has already more than redeemed the promise that his most sanguine friends made in his behalf on his first appearance as a writer. There are poems in the present volume which any American writer might be proud to own. We call the attention of the reader to "The Fountain in Winter," "The Pine Forest of Monterey," "Sorrowful Music," and "The Metempsychosis of the Pine," in support of our opinion. The ballad of "Manuela" is full of picturesque beauty of description, and has the genuine tenderness of Nature. If it had no other merit, it would deserve honorable mention as the foundation of that admirable parody, "The Ballad of Martha Hopkins," which is every way the best specimen of an American idyl we have yet met with. The energetic and enterprising author of these poems is now on his way to Nineveh, and thence to that unsearched goal of the world's travellers, the true source of the Nile. No idle dreamer, but a man of action, as well as thought; if his life and health are spared a few years longer, he will leave his mark upon his age, not merely as a gifted poet, but as a brave and successful explorer of the dark places of the earth.

J. G. W.

National Era, Washington, November 6, 1851.

GREENWOOD LEAVES

(Second Series)

The first volume of these pleasant miscellanies, published a year or two since, has passed through two large editions, and prepared the way for the favorable reception of the one now before us; yet any judgment of this volume, founded upon a knowledge of the former one, would scarcely do it justice. Its tales and sketches are higher-toned, evincing a clearer eye to the realities of things; a more accurate hand is discernible in the delineation of character, and in the descriptive passages.

We are confident, however, that the reading public will agree
with us, that by far the best portion of the volume is that devoted
to the racy and familiar letters, from town and country, many of
which were originally addressed to the editor of the *Era.* We
scarcely know anything better, in the whole range of epistolary
literature. Fresh, sparkling, hopeful, electric with life, dealing
with men and things with the freest possible play of fancy and
wit, yet always with good humor and kindness — alike happy in
describing a horseback gallop in the woods or a debate in Congress, Jenny Lind's music or Webster's oratory, Brackett's
immortal marbles or the cold points in the *physique* of some
Congressional notability — they have all the spirit and vivacity
of Lady Mary Wortley Montague's letters, while they are happily
without the bitterness of sarcasm and defective moral sense of
those remarkable productions. She never forgets her account-
ability to the Great Giver for the use of her talents. Amidst all
her playfulness, freedom, and gaiety — in her grave or cheerful
moods, in her indignant rebukes of wrong, and her enthusiastic
admiration of the good and noble traits of human character and
action, the great idea of duty is always visible. Although entirely
fearless in her advocacy of unpopular truths, she is no fanatic,
and seldom violates the proprieties of time and audience by
intruding her opinions, while she is careful to lose no proper
opportunity for saying a good word for freedom and humanity.
That a rigid, critical analysis of her writings might call attention
to certain faults of style and taste is very possible; but, secure
as she is of popular favor, she can well afford to listen to the
complaints of "word-catchers who live on syllables" with the
cool complacency of Sir John Harrington:

> "The readers and the hearers like my books.
>   But yet some critics cannot them digest;
>   But what care I? For, when I make a feast,
> I would my guests should praise it, not the cooks."

J. G. W.

National Era, Washington, January 29, 1852.

THE WHITE SLAVE: OR
MEMOIRS OF A FUGITIVE

We opened this volume not without some fears that we should find it a weak imitation of the highly successful and powerful romance of *Harriet Beecher Stowe*. We were by no means willing to see that marvellous picture copied, and, as a matter of course, caricatured by a second-rate artist. But the author of this book is no copyist. He has stamped it with originality as marked, and in its way as effective, as that of "Uncle Tom's Cabin." It lacks the admirable painting of negro character, the mingled pathos and drollery of that remarkable book. Its author seems to have studied human nature in classes rather than in individuals--the current of its narrative runs strongly but evenly; its scenes and conversations are not calculated for dramatic effect. It is the story of a slave, and it is the slave in middle life, educated, refined, wealthy, and free, who tells it. With him, life had been grave and earnest, and such is his narrative. It has the stern and stately movement of the old Greek tragedy.

As a picture of slavery, in its moral, social, and political bearing, upon the north as well as the South, it furnishes hints and facts which are overlooked in Uncle Tom's Cabin. In truth, apart from their subject, there is little or nothing in common between the two books. In purer raciness, sprightliness, and picturesque effect, Uncle Tom's Cabin has greatly the advantage. In the style of the author before us, everything is subdued and sombered. His refined passion and steady energy reminds us of Godwin in Caleb Williams and St. Leon. The high reputation he has received in another department of literature will not suffer by his present production, which deserves and will have a wide circulation. Its success will not affect in any degree the popular demand for the extraordinary work of his female co-laborer in the new and rich field of American romance — "Life among the Lowly."

J. G. W.

National Era, Washington, August 5, 1852.

WAVERLEY NOVELS

The new edition of the Waverley Novels, published by S.H. Parker and B. B. Mussey and Co., Boston, is decidedly the best ever published in America. Each volume contains a complete novel. These books are of duodecimo size; the paper is good, the type large and handsome, and the press-work clearly done. The binding is strong and elegant, and each volume has two illustrations. It is a superior edition, and the price is as low as the worst. We are sure we speak for thousands, when we welcome these charming volumes. We have experienced real pleasure in turning over their clear pages, and remembering how they bewitched us years ago. We love to linger over some familiar scene, and think how our heart beat with the wildest romance as we gave ourself wholly to the sweet glamour of the story. Again our old heroes, all "plaided and plumed," step forth into the present sunshine. We see the procession pass — a little sadly, it may be; for though they were once living, breathing beings, they are now a shade ghost-like, seen through the mist of years:

"With coronach and arms reversed, forth comes Mac Gregor's clan,
Red Dougal's cry peals shrill and wild, Rob Roy's bold brow
looks wan;
On Sweep Bois Guilbert, Front de Boeuf, De Bracy's plume of wo,
And Coeur de Lion's crest shines near the valiant Ivanhoe.

Balfour of Burley, Claverhouse, the Lord of Evandale,
And stately Lady Margaret, whose might nought avail;
Fierce Rothwell, on his charger black, as from the conflict won;
And pale Habakkuk Muckelwrath, who cried, 'God's will be done!'

And, like a rose, a young white rose, that blooms mid wildest
scenes,
Comes she, the modest, eloquent, and virtuous Jeanie Deans;
And Dumbeidikes, the silent laird, with love too deep to smile;
And Effie, with her noble friend, the good Duke of Argyle."

The binding of the volumes is appropriate, as well as ornamental. On one side is stamped the head of Sir Walter Scott; on the reverse is Abbotsford. On the back, is the author's coat of arms.

This edition is to be completed in twenty-four volumes, at the low price of $15.00 for the whole series.

National Era, Washington, November 4, 1852.

THALATTA: A BOOK FOR THE SEA SIDE

Under this title, suggested by a passage in Xenophon's Expedition of Cyrus, where the army climbed the hill and looked out upon the sea, throwing up their arms and shouting, "Thalatta! Thalatta!" we have here an admirable collection of poems more or less intimately connected with the ocean and its adjuncts. The writers are of all ages and localities from Homer to Longfellow—from Spain to Massachusetts. The selections have been made with good taste and judgement, and will be found pleasant reading, not only by sojourners at the sea side during our hot season, but also by those who are compelled to forego the pleasure of a ride on Nahant, or a bath at Newport. To these latter, sweltering in their inland homes, we would especially commend this little volume. It is redolent of the salt sea breezes. It can scarcely fail to transport its readers from hot prairie or dusty city to the cool margin of great waters—making everything about them, as on Prosper's Island, "Suffer a sea change."

Among our old favorites in this volume is what Coleridge has well called "The Grand Ballad of Sir Patrick Spens." Nothing superior to it can be found in all the quaint old ballad literature, and no modern imitation has ever equalled its simple grandeur, picturesque descriptions, and dramatic energy.

"The ladyes wrang their fingers white,
The maidens tore their hair;

191

A' for the sake o' their true loves,
For them they'll see nae mair!

O lang lang may the ladyes sit,
Wi' their faces in their hand,
Before they see Sir Patrick Spens
Come sailing to the strand!

And lang, lang may the maidens sit,
Wi' their gold kames in their hair,
A-waiting for their ain true loves
For them they'll see nae mair!"

Here are also Goethe's "Fisher," Uhland's weird and beautiful "Vineta," and Shelley's pathetic lament at the Bay of Naples. Among the novelties may be mentioned two or three rare gems from Allingham, the gifted young Milesian poet, and two remarkable little sea sketches from the pen of Charles Kingsley, author of Alton Locke.

The following song, in its simple reality of pathos, might well have been sung around a fisherman's hearth on the shore of Dee, to the drear accompaniment of the growing roar of the evening tide, over-sweeping the sands with its "cruel, hungry foam:"

"Oh! Mary, go and call the cattle home,
And call the cattle home—
And call the cattle home—
Across the sands of Dee;
The Western wind was wild and dank wi' foam,
And all alone went she.

The creeping tide came up along the sand,
And o'er and o'er the sand—
And round and round the sand—
As far as eye could see
The blinding mist came down and hid the land,
And never home came she.

Oh! Is it weed, or fish, or floating hair,
   A tress of golden hair
   O' drowned maiden's hair—
Above the nets at sea?
Was never salmon yet that shone so fair,
   Among the stakes of Dee!

They rowed her in across the rolling foam,
   The cruel crawling foam—
   The cruel hungry foam—
To her grave beside the sea;
But still the boatmen hear her call the cattle home,
   Across the sands of Dee!"

We cannot resist the desire to copy the following sea-side picture by Allingham.

THE CHAPEL BY THE SHORE

"By the shore a plot of ground
Clips a ruined chapel round,
Buttressed with a grassy mound,
   Where day and night and day go by,
And bring no touch of human sound.

Washing of the lonely seas—
Shaking of the guardian trees—
Piping of the salted breeze—
   And day and night and day go by,
To the endless tone of these.

Or when winds and waters keep
A hush more dead than any sleep,
Still morns to stiller evenings creep
   And day and night and day go by,
Here the stillness is most deep.

And the ruins lapsed again
Into nature's wide domain,

193

Sow themselves with seed and grain
    As night and day and night go by,
And hoard June's sun and April's rain.

    Here fresh funeral tears were shed,
    But now the graves are also dead;
    And suckers from the ash tree spread,
        As day and night and day go by,
    And stars move calmly overhead!"

The book is got up in the usual good taste of the firm by which
it is published. It will be found a pleasant traveling companion,
and a seasonable addition to warm-weather readings.

J. G. W.

National Era, Washington, July 14, 1853.

BAYARD TAYLOR

Our readers, we feel certain, will thank us for calling their
attention to Ticknor and Fields' new and revised edition of
Bayard Taylor's *Poems of Home and Travel.* All the admirable
characteristics of the author's prose are reproduced in these
picturesque and most felicitous verses. Those suggested by his
world-wide rambles have for us a peculiar interest. Their pictures are from life—clear, vivid, genial, and truthful. They have
the breadth, freedom, and resonance, of air and sky, and ocean—
the pine forests of Monterey answering the solemn roll of the
Pacific—the wild Styrian mountains and limitless savannas of the
West. In this volume, as in all the writings of the author, one
feels the healthful warmth and vigorous pulsations of a strong,
brave, and beautiful life, in which romance and adventure are
tempered by an abiding sense of moral obligation, and that charity and kindly sympathy with human life, in all its phases, which
mark the travelled gentleman and Christian cosmopolitan.

J. G. W.

National Era, Washington, May 1, 1856

POEMS BY LUCY LARCOM

Whittier's Estimate of Them*

In issuing this volume of Miss Larcom's Poems the Publishers invite attention to the following expression of opinions by the poet, Whittier:

"The announcement of a volume from the pen of Lucy Larcom will be welcomed by her many admirers in all parts of the country. Having had an opportunity to look over a portion of the manuscript, I do not hesitate to predict for the book a permanent popularity. Its author holds in rare combination the healthfulness of simple truth and common sense, with a fine and delicate fancy, and an artist's perception of all beauty. Wholly without cant, affectation, or imitation, the moral tone of the serious poems is noteworthy. The religious sentiment of New England never had a more winning and graceful interpreter, for she has succeeded in reconciling Puritanism with the liberal and yet reverent spirit of modern inquiry. Her ballads have the true flavor and feeling of the breezy New England sea-coast."

Fields, Osgood & Co., Publishers. Boston,1868

*A broadside advertising leaflet.

Editor's Preface

to

CHILD LIFE: A COLLECTION OF POEMS

Having had occasion, some time since, to look over several volumes of selected verse intended for juvenile readers, and noticing in nearly all of them much that seemed lacking in literary merit or adaptation, it occurred to the compiler of this volume that, taking advantage of the merits as well as deficiencies of existing publications in this department, a selection might be made combining simplicity with a certain degree of literary excellence, without on the one hand descending to silliness, or, on the other rising above the average comprehension of childhood.

How far the present volume has made this thought a reality it is not for him to decide. He can only say that it is the result of patient examination of the accessible juvenile literature of our own and other countries. Our English tongue is peculiarly rich in the lore of home and fireside; and the editor has availed himself of selections from folk-songs and ballads of continental Europe. Where a doubt existed in regard to any particular poem he has not hesitated to take counsel of those whose judgment seemed to him reliable; and, in more than one instance, he has deferred to the instinctive and natural criticisms of childhood.

It is but just to acknowledge his obligations to kind friends whose valuable suggestions have materially aided him; and, in an especial manner, his indebtedness to *Lucy Larcom,* so well known in connexion with *"Our Young Folks,"* who has given him the benefit of her cultivated taste and very thorough acquaintance with whatever is valuable in the poetical literature of Child Life.

Doubtless all readers will miss some favorite pieces which the necessity of giving as great variety as possible to the compilation compelled him to pass over. He trusts, however, that a very large proportion of all that is permanently valuable will be found in these pages. He hopes and believes that no well-grounded exceptions can be taken to the character of the selections in a moral and religious point of view. He has endeavored, avoiding everything like cant and sectarianism, to find expression for the reverence, love, and grateful trust, so natural and beautiful in those whom the Divine Teacher held up as examples to His disciples: "Of such is the kingdom of Heaven." The deep significance of His language is confirmed by the spiritual experience of all ages.

"The paths that lead us to God's throne
Are worn by children's feet."

In the department of hymns and strictly devotional pieces, the number which seemed really appropriate in language and thought proved, on examination, to be much smaller than was anticipated. Something more perhaps might have been added from Watts and Jane Taylor, but the one beautiful hymn of Faber, with which the volume closes, contains in itself the substance and spirit of all.

Of course, fancy and imagination must play a prominent part in such a compilation, as they do in all healthful young minds, but the editor trusts that little will be found which can, by any possibility, leave an impression of evil, or really confuse the distinctions of truth and error. Even pure nonsense, as in the case of Lear's "Owl and Pussy Cat," may not be without a certain moral value as a fitting caricature of the affectation of sentiment. In Hauff's "Fortunes of Fairy-Lore," the heroine complains, to her mother Fancy, that the world has grown uncomfortably wise, and that the very children who used to love her so dearly have become too knowing for their tender age, and, no longer capable of wonder, laugh at her stories and turn their backs upon her. Poor Fairy-Lore is doubtless justified in her complaint,—the school-master and newspaper are busy with their disenchantments, —but, as there may be still left among us something of that beautiful unwisdom which once peopled the child's world with visionary shapes, it should have the benefit of such poems as Mary Howitts's "Caldon Low," Allingham's "Fairies," and Allan Cunningham's "Song of the Elfin Miller."

While the compiler has endeavored to accommodate his book to the especial tastes of the young, he has not been without hope maturer readers may find something of interest in it, —something to bring back the freshness of the past, —hints and echoes from the lost world of childhood. He is happy in believing that, in this way, some noontide wayfarer may be able to discover shadowy places of memory where the dew of the morning of life has not wholly dried up, and where may still be heard the music of the birds of sunrise.

Sincerely hoping that in the selection of these poems of Child-Life, he has not altogether misunderstood the tastes, wishes, and needs of his young readers; he leaves it in their hands, commending to each of them the words of one who has himself written well and wisely for their class:

> "Be good dear child, and let who will be clever
> Do noble things, not dream them, all day long;
> And so make life, death, and that vast forever
> One grand sweet song."

J. G. W.

Amesbury, 4th Month, 1871

Editor's Preface

To

CHILD LIFE IN PROSE

The unexpectedly favorable reception of the poetical compilation entitled "Child Life" has induced its publishers to call for the preparation of a companion volume of prose stories and sketches, gathered, like the former, from the literature of widely separated nationalities and periods. Illness, preoccupation, and the inertia of unelastic years would have deterred me from the undertaking, but for the assistance which I have had from the lady whose services are acknowledged in the preface to "Child Life." I beg my young readers, therefore, to understand that I claim little credit for my share in the work, since whatever merit it may have is largely due to her taste and judgment. It may be well to admit, in the outset, that the book is as much for child-lovers, who have not outgrown their child-heartedness in becoming mere men and women, as for children themselves; that it is as much *about* childhood, as *for* it. If not the wisest, it appears to me that the happiest people in the world are those who still retain something of the child's creative faculty of imagination, which makes atmosphere and color, sun and shadow, and boundless horizons, out of what seems to prosaic wisdom most inadequate material,—a tuft of grass, a mossy rock, the rain-pools

198

of a passing shower, a glimpse of sky and cloud, a waft of west-wind, a bird's flutter and song. For the child is always something of a poet; if he cannot analyze, like Wordsworth and Tennyson, the emotions which expand his being, even as the fulness of life bursts open the petals of a flower, he finds with them all Nature plastic to his eye and hand. The soul of genius and the heart of childhood are one.

Not irreverently has Jean Paul said, "I love God and little children. Ye stand nearest to Him, ye little ones." From the Infinite Heart a sacred Presence has gone forth and filled the earth with the sweetness of immortal infancy. Not once in history alone, but every day and always, Christ sets the little child in the midst of us as the truest reminder of himself, teaching us the secret of happiness, and leading us into the kingdom by the way of humility and tenderness.

In truth, all the sympathies of our nature combine to render childhood an object of powerful interest. Its beauty, innocence, dependence, and possibilities of destiny, strongly appeal to our sensibilities, not only in real life, but in fiction and poetry. How sweetly, admist the questionable personages who give small occasion of respect for manhood or womanhood as they waltz and wander through the story of Wilhelm Meister, rises the child-figure of Mignon! How we turn from the light dames and faithless cavaliers of Boccaccio to contemplate his exquisite picture of the little Florentine, Beatrice, that fair girl of eight summers, so "pretty in her childish ways, so ladylike and pleasing, with her delicate features and fair proportions, of such dignity and charm of manner as to be looked upon as a little angel!" And of all the creations of her illustrious lover's genius, whether in the world of mortals or in the uninviting splendors of his Para-dise, what is there so beautiful as the glimpse we have of him in his *Vita Nuova*, a boy of nine years, amidst the bloom and greenness of the Spring Festival of Florence, checking his noisy merry-making in rapt admiration of the little Beatrice, who seemed to him "not the daughter of mortal man, but of God"? Who does not thank John Brown, of Edinburgh, for the story of Marjorie Fleming, the fascinating child-woman, laughing beneath the plaid of Walter Scott, and gathering at her feet the wit and genius of Scotland? The labored essays from which St. Pierre hoped for

199

immortality, his philosophies, sentimentalisms, and theories of tides, have all quietly passed into the limbo of unreadable things; while a simple story of childhood keeps his memory green as the tropic island in which the scene is laid, and his lovely creations remain to walk hand in hand beneath the palms of Mauritius so long as children shall be born and the hearts of youths and maidens cleave to each other. If the after story of the poet-king and warrior of Israel sometimes saddens and pains us, who does not love to think of him as a shepherd boy, "ruddy and withal of a beautiful countenance, and goodly to look upon," singing to his flocks on the hill-slopes of Bethlehem?

In the compilation of this volume the chief embarrassment has arisen from the very richness and abundance of materials. As a matter of course, the limitations prescribed by its publishers have compelled the omission of much that, in point of merit, may compare favorably with the selections. Dickens' great family of ideal children, Little Nell, Tiny Tim, and the Marchioness; Harriet Beecher Stowe's Eva and Topsy; George Macdonald's quaint and charming child-dreamers; and last, but not least, John Brown's Pet Marjorie,—are only a few of the pictures for which no place has been found. The book, of necessity, but imperfectly reflects that child-world which fortunately is always about us, more beautiful in its living realities than it has ever been painted.

It has been my wish to make a readable book of such literary merit as not to offend the cultivated taste of parents, while it amused their children. I may confess in this connection, that, while aiming at simple and not unhealthful amusement, I have been glad to find the light tissue of these selections occasionally shot through with threads of pious or moral suggestion. At the same time, I have not felt it right to sadden my child-readers with gloomy narratives and painful reflections upon the life before them. The lessons taught are those of Love, rather than Fear. "I can bear," said Richter, "to look upon a melancholy man, but I cannot look upon a melancholy child. Fancy a butterfly crawling like a caterpillar with his four wings pulled off!"

It is possible that the language and thought of some portions of the book may be considered beyond the comprehension of the class for which it is intended. Admitting that there may be truth in the objection, I believe with Coventry Patmore, in his preface to a child's book, that the charm of such a volume is increased, rather than lessened, by the surmised existence of an unknown amount of power, meaning, and beauty. I well remember how, at a very early age, the solemn organ-roll of Gray's Elegy and the lyric sweep and pathos of Cowper's Lament for the Royal George moved and fascinated me with a sense of mystery and power felt, rather than understood. "A Spirit passed before my face, but the form thereof was not discerned." Freighted with un-guessed meanings, these poems spake to me, in an unknown tongue indeed, but, like the wind in the pines or the waves on the beach, awakening faint echoes and responses, and vaguely prophesying of wonders yet to be revealed. John Woolman tells us, in his autobiography, that, when a small child, he read from that sacred prose poem, the Book of Revelation, which has so perplexed critics and commentators, these words, "He showed me a river of the waters of life clear as crystal, proceeding out of the throne of God and the Lamb." and that his mind was drawn thereby to seek after that wonderful purity, and that the place where he sat and the sweetness of that child-yearning remained still fresh in his memory in after life. The spirit of that mystical anthem which Milton speaks of as "a seven-fold chorus of hallelujahs and harping symphonies," hidden so often from the wise and prudent students of the letter, was felt, if not comprehended, by the simple heart of the child.

It will be seen that a considerable portion of the volume is devoted to autobiographical sketches of infancy and childhood. It seemed to me that it might be interesting to know how the dim gray dawn and golden sunrise of life looked to poets and phil-osophers; and to review with them the memories upon which the reflected light of their genius has fallen.

I leave the little collection, not without some misgivings, to the critical, but I hope not unkindly, regard of its young readers. They will, I am sure, believe me when I tell them that if my own paternal claims, like those of Elia, are limited to "dream child-dren," I have catered for the real ones with cordial sympathy and tender solicitude for their well-being and happiness.

Amesbury, 1873   J. G. W.

Preface to

SONGS OF THREE CENTURIES

Edited by

John Greenleaf Whittier

It would be doing injustice to the compiler of this volume to suppose that his work implied any lack of appreciation of the excellent anthologies already published in this country. Dana's "Household Book of Poetry" is no misnomer; and the honored names of Bryant and Emerson are a sufficient guaranty for "Parnassus" and the "Library of Song." With no thought of superseding or even of entering into direct competition with these large and valuable collections, it has been my design to gather up in a comparatively small volume, easily accessible to all classes of readers, the wisest thoughts, rarest fancies, and devoutest hymns of the metrical authors of the last three centuries. To use Shelley's definition of poetry, I have endeavored to give something like "a record of the best thoughts and happiest moments of the best and happiest minds." The plan of my work has compelled me to confine myself, in a great measure, to the lyrical productions of the authors quoted, and to use only the briefer poems of the old dramatists and such voluminous writers as Spenser, Milton, Dryden, Cowper, Pope, Bryon, Scott, Wordsworth, and the Brownings. Of course, no anthology, however ample its extracts, could do justice to the illimitable genius of Shakespeare.

It is possible that it may be thought an undue prominence has been given to the poetry of the period beginning with Cowper and reaching down to Tennyson and his living contemporaries. But it must be considered that the last century has been prolific in song; and, if Shakespeare and Milton still keep their unapproachable position, "souls like stars that dwell apart," there can be little doubt that the critical essayist of the twentieth century will make a large advance upon the present estimate, not only of Cowper and Burns, but of Wordsworth, Coleridge, Shelley,

Keats, Browning, Tennyson, and Emerson.

It will be seen that the middle of the sixteenth century is the earliest date of my citations. The great name of Chaucer does not appear; and some of the best of the early ballad poetry of England and Scotland has been reluctantly omitted. James I., whose Queen's Quhair, has hidden his kingly crown under the poet's garland, William Dunbar, and Sackville, Earl of Dorset, may well be thought worthy of a place in any collection of English verse, but the language and rhythm of these writers render them wellnigh unintelligible to the ordinary reader.

The selections I have made indicate, in a general way, my preferences; but I have not felt at liberty to oppose my own judgment or prejudice to the best critical authorities, or to attempt a reversal of the verdicts of Time. It would be too much to hope that I have, in all cases, made the best possible exposition of an author's productions. Judging from my own experience in looking over selected poems, I cannot doubt that my readers will often have occasion to question the wisdom of my choice, and regret the omission of favorite pieces. It is rarely that persons of equal capacity for right judging can be found to coincide entirely in regard to the merits of a particular poem. The canons of criticism are by no means fixed and infallible; and the fashion of poetry, like that of the world, "passeth away." Not only every age, but every reader, holds the right of private judgment. It would be difficult for any literary inquisitor-general to render a good reason for condemning as a heretic the man who finds the "Castle of Indolence" pleasanter reading than the "Faerie Queene," who prefers Cowper to Dryden, Scott to Byron, and Shelley to Scott, who passes by Moore's "Lalla Rookh" to to take up Clough's "Bothie of Tober-na Vuolich," who thinks Emerson's "Threnody" better than Milton's "Lycidas," and who would not exchange a good old ballad or a song of Burns for the stateliest of epics.

The considerable space which I have given to American authors will, I trust, find its justification in the citations from their writings. The poetical literature of our country can scarcely be said to have a longer date than that of a single generation. As a matter of fact, the very fathers of it are still living. It really commenced with Bryant's "Thanatopsis" and Dana's "Buccaneer." The grave, philosophic tone, chaste simplicity of language, freedom of versification, and freshness and truth of illustration, which marked the former poem, and the terse realism of the "Buccaneer," with its stern pictures of life and nature drawn with few strokes sharp and vigorous as those of Retzsch's outlines, left the weak imitators of an artificial school without an audience. All further attempts to colonize the hills and pastures of New England from old mythologies were abandoned; our boys and girls no longer figured in impossible pastorals. If we have no longer ambitious Columbiads and Conquests of Canaan, we have at least truth and nature, wit and wisdom, in Bryant's "Robert of Lincoln," Emerson's "Humblebee," Lowell's "Courtin'," and "The One-Hoss Shay" of Holmes.

In dealing with contemporary writers I have found myself embarrassed by the very large number of really noticeable poems, many of which, although in my own estimation vastly better than those of some of the old versifiers whose age and general reputation have secured them a place in this volume, I have been compelled to omit solely from lack of space. The future gleaner in the fields over which I have passed will doubtless find many an ungarnered sheaf quite as well worth preserving as these I have gathered within the scanty limits of my compendium. The rare humorists of our time, especially such poets as Holmes and Lowell, can be only partially represented in these necessarily brief selections.

It may be observed that the three divisions of the book do not strictly correspond to the headings which indicate them,—the first, for instance, beginning before Shakespeare and ending somewhat after Milton. It is difficult to be quite exact in such classifications; and as it seemed desirable to make their number as small as possible. I trust the few leading names mentioned may serve to characterize the periods they accompany with a sufficient degree of accuracy. Pope was doubtless the great master of what is sometimes spoken of as artificial verse, shaping the mould of poetic thought for his own and the succeeding generation; but as Dryden stands in point of time nearer to the colossal name which closes the first period of English song, he has been chosen as a representative of the second, in connection and contrast with Burns, who, in his vigorous rebound from the measured pomp of rhymed heroics to the sturdiest and homeliest Scottish simplicity, gave to the modern lyric its inspiration, striking for the age the musical pitch of true and tender emotion, as decidedly as Wordsworth has touched for it the keynote of the thoughtful harmonies of natural and intellectual beauty. Tennyson undoubtedly stands at the head of all living singers, and his name might well serve as the high-water mark of modern verse; but, as our volume gives a liberal space to American authorship, I have ventured to let the name of the author of "Evangeline" represent, as it well may, the present poetic culture of our English-speaking people at home and abroad.

While by no means holding myself to a strict responsibility as regards the sentiment and language of the poems which make up this volume, and while I must confess to a large tolerance of personal individuality manifesting itself in widely varying forms of expression, I have still somewhat scrupulously endeavored to avoid in my selections everything which seemed liable to the charge of irreverence or questionable morality. In this respect the poetry of the last quarter of a century, with a few exceptions, has been noteworthy for purity of thought and language, as well as for earnestness and religious feeling. The Muse of our time is a free but profoundly reverent inquirer; it is rarely found in "the seat of the scorner." If it does not always speak in the prescribed language of creed and formula, its utterances often give evidence of fresh communion with that Eternal Spirit whose responses are never in any age or clime withheld from the devout questioner.

My great effort has been to make a thoroughly readable book. With this in view I have not given tedious extracts from dull plays and weary epics, but have gathered up the best of the old ballads and short, time-approved poems, and drawn largely from contemporary writers and the waifs and estrays of unknown authors. I have also, as a specialty of the work, made a careful selection of the best hymns in our language. I am prepared to find my method open to criticism from some quarters, but I have catered not so much for the scholarly few as for the great mass of readers to whose "snatched leisure" my brief lyrical selections would seem to have a special adaptation.

It only remains for me to acknowledge the valuable suggestions and aid I have received from various sources during the preparation of this volume, and especially the essential assistance I have had from Lucy Larcom of Beverly Farms, to whose services I have before been indebted in the compilation of "Child Life."

J. G. W.

Amesbury, 9th mo., 1875

EMERSON'S BIRTHDAY

Whittier joined Whitman, G.W. Curtis, T.W. Higginson and others in celebrating Emerson's birthday in 1880. His is merely a short note which follows several articles.

No words of mine can overstate my respect and admiration for the great poet and essayist whose seventy-seventh birthday the *Literary World* does well to honor. Standing as he does at the head of our literature, and foremost among the philosophical thinkers of our age, it needs no gift of prophecy to foresee that his reputation will lose nothing by the lapse of time. No living poet of the English-speaking tongue has written verses bearing more distinctly than his the mark of immortality. In his prose works all must recognize his keen insight, wisdom, fine sense of humor, large tolerance, and love of nature in her simplest as well as grandest aspects—an inimitable combination of practical sagacity, profound reflection and mystical intuition. May his days be long in the land!

John G. Whittier

The Literary World, Boston, May 22, 1880

PREFACE

NINETEEN BEAUTIFUL YEARS

With preface by

John Greenleaf Whittier

Francis E. Willard, Chicago, 1885

The impression made on me by the perusal of the first edition of this little book has not been weakened by the lapse of time. It seems to me now, as it did then, a very sweet and tender record of the exceptionally beautiful life of a young woman whose rare natural gifts and graces were sanctified by a deep, but cheerful and healthful religious experience, free from cant, affectation or bigotry. It is an attractive picture of the "sweet reasonableness" of Christian development—a lovely human character flowering into the beauty of holiness. The story is told by her sister, Francis E. Willard, so widely known and honored for her work of Christian philanthropy. It is a charming piece of biography, and it would be well if it would take the place of many well-meant but unwholesome tracts and memoirs now in circulation, the tendency of which is to depress rather than to encourage and strengthen the seeker after a better life.

John G. Whittier

Amesbury, 4th month 4, 1885

CHECK LIST OF WHITTIER CRITICAL ARTICLES NOT GATHERED INTO THE COLLECTED WRITINGS

Page

The National Era, Washington, D.C.

"natural revulsion from the unsatisfying dreams of sentimentalism to the homely but substantial joys of commonplace life."

New Books   No critical value
    July 6, 1854
Bayard Taylor   194
    May 1, 1856

Poems by Lucy Larcom. Whittier's Estimate of Them.   195
    Advertising leaflet of Fields, Osgood and Co.,
    Boston, 1868

Boston Evening Transcript
    Letter commending *Littell's Living Age.*
        April 5, 1858. Praise for balance, comprehensiveness,
        equality with best British periodicals.
    Birthday Greetings to Oliver Wendell Holmes
        August 31, 1885

Century Magazine
    Letter on J.G. Holland
        January, 1882. Expressing grief at the death of author
        whose writings were marked by "practical wisdom, broad
        Christian charity, earnest patriotism, and crystal purity..."
    On Copyright
        February, 1886. Favors International Copyright on moral
        grounds.

Boatswain's Whistle, Boston
    John Woolman in the Steerage
        November 17, 1864
        The story of Woolman's testimony against the injustices
        done eighteenth century sailors which made him go steer-
        age rather than cabin-passage to England. Illustrates sym-
        pathetically other Woolman "concerns" against slavery,
        pride, oppression, and avarice. Holds that Woolman pre-
        dicted the horrors of the Civil War in prophesying divine
        retribution for the evils of slavery.

Preface to *Child Life: A Collection of Poems,* 1871   195

Preface to *Child Life in Prose,* 1874   196

INDEX

217